Great American Writers
TWENTIETH CENTURY

EDITOR

R. BAIRD SHUMAN

University of Illinois

Eudora Welty • Edith Wharton

Thornton Wilder • Tennessee Williams • William Carlos Williams

Richard Wright • Paul Zindel

MARSHALL CAVENDISH

NEW YORK • TORONTO • LONDON • SYDNEY

Marshall Cavendish
99 White Plains Road
Tarrytown, New York 10591-9001

Website: www.marshallcavendish.com

Salem Press

    Editor: R. Baird Shuman
    Managing Editor: R. Kent Rasmussen

    Manuscript Editors: Heather Stratton
                       Lauren M. Mitchell
    Assistant Editor: Andrea Miller
    Research Supervisor: Jeffry Jensen
    Acquisitions Editor: Mark Rehn

Marshall Cavendish

    Project Editor: Marian Armstrong
    Editorial Director: Paul Bernabeo

Designer: Patrice Sheridan

Photo Research: Candlepants
                  Carousel Research
                  Linda Sykes Picture Research
                  Anne Burns Images

Indexing: AEIOU

Library of Congress Cataloging-in-Publication Data

Great American writers: twentieth century / R. Baird Shuman, editor.
    v. cm.
    Includes bibliographical references and indexes.
    Contents: v. 1. Agee-Bellow--v. 2. Benét-Cather--v. 3. Cormier-
Dylan--v. 4. Eliot-Frost--v. 5. Gaines-Hinton--v. 6. Hughes-Lewis--v. 7.
London-McNickle--v. 8. Miller-O'Connor--v. 9. O'Neill-Rich--v. 10.
Salinger-Stein--v. 11. Steinbeck-Walker--v. 12. Welty-Zindel--v. 13.
Index.
    ISBN 0-7614-7240-1 (set)—ISBN 0-7614-7252-5 (v. 12)
    1. American literature--20th century--Bio-bibliography--
Dictionaries. 2. Authors, American--20th century--Biography--
Dictionaries. 3. American literature--20th century--Dictionaries. I.
Shuman, R. Baird (Robert Baird), 1929-

PS221.G74 2002
810.9'005'03
[B]   2001028461

Printed in Malaysia; bound in the United States

07 06 05 04 03 02   6 5 4 3 2 1

Volume 12 Illustration Credits
(a = above, b = below, l = left, r = right)

 The Andy Warhol Foundation, Inc./Art Resource, NY: 1723
Astrakhan Art Gallery, Russia/SuperStock: 1600
Barnes and Noble Publishing: 1615
The Beinecke Rare Book and Manuscript Library, Yale Collection of
American Literature, Yale University: cover portrait of Richard Wright,
1613, 1614, 1619, 1627, 1630, 1693, 1694, 1696 (a), 1709
Bridgeman Art Library: 1643
Bridgeman Art Library/Mallett and Son Antiques, Ltd., London, UK:
1601
Julia Condon/SuperStock: 1699
Corbis: cover portrait of Eudora Welty, cover portrait of Tennessee
Williams, 1589, 1651, 1696 (b), 1701, 1705
Corbis/Bettmann: cover portrait of Edith Wharton, cover portrait of
Thornton Wilder, 1611, 1612, 1616, 1629, 1638, 1695, 1698, 1700,
1717
Corbis/Pach Brothers: cover portrait of William Carlos Williams,
1675, 1678
Fine Art Photographic Library, London/Art Resource: 1625
Giraudon/Art Resource, NY: 1635, 1690
Grand Design/SuperStock: 1680
Harcourt Brace & Company: 1596
HarperCollins Publishers: 1634, 1647
Photography Collection at Harry Ransome Humanities Research
Center, The University of Texas at Austin: 1652, 1653, 1655, 1657,
1658, 1659, 1660
Hulton/Archive Photos: 1591, 1631, 1684
Hulton Deutch Collection/Corbis: 1682
Lawrenceville School: 1631
Erich Lessing/Art Resource, NY: 1595, 1648, 1665, 1681, 1691
Private Collection/Hyacinth Manning/SuperStock: 1605
Metropolitan Museum of Art/SuperStock: 1594
Mississippi Department of Archives and History: 1590, 1606
Museum of the City of New York/Corbis: 1618
Courtesy of New Directions: 1679, 1686
The Newark Museum/Art Resource, NY: 1609, 1689
New Jersey Historical Society: 1676, 1685
From the Paul Zindel Collection Department of Special Collections,
Boston University: 1713, 1714
Penguin Books: 1654, 1664
Photofest: 1636, 1640, 1642, 1646, 1649, 1656, 1661, 1667, 1669,
1671, 1672, 1718, 1720
Private Collection, Christian Pierre/SuperStock: 1716
From *The Effect of Gamma Rays on Man-in-the-Moon Marigolds* (Jacket
Cover) by Paul Zindel. Used by permission of Bantam Books, a divi-
sion of Random House, Inc.: 1721
From *The Pigman* (Jacket Cover Only) by Paul Zindel. Used by per-
mission of Bantam Books, a division of Random House, Inc.: 1722
Roger Ressmeyer/Corbis: cover portrait of Paul Zindel, 1711, 1715
Réunion des Musées Nationaux/Art Resource, NY: 1621, 1623, 1673
Scala/Art Resource, NY: 1725
Nancy R. Schiff/Archive Photos: 1599
Smithsonian American Art Museum, Washington, D.C./Art Resource,
NY: 1603, 1645, 1688, 1702, 1706, 1708
P.L. Sperr/Archive Photos: 1712
Cecil Stoughton/L.B.J. Library: 1633
SuperStock: 1607
United States Post Office: 1637
University of Pennsylvania Archives and Record Center: 1677
The University of Wisconsin Archives: 1592

Contents

Eudora Welty

BORN: April 13, 1909, Jackson, Mississippi
DIED: July 23, 2001, Jackson, Mississippi
IDENTIFICATION: Mid-twentieth-century southern writer who advanced the short story as a literary form in its own right.

Perhaps Eudora Welty's most significant achievement was her creating a separate literary niche apart from that of fellow Mississippian William Faulkner, who otherwise dominated the southern literary scene at that time. Known for her southern settings, her attention to detail, her sense of humor, and her vivid characterizations, Welty is arguably one of the greatest writers of southern fiction. As much as she credited the importance of place, particularly her local Mississippi landscape, in her fiction, her real subjects were always human relationships, especially within families. She wrote the bulk of her short stories in the 1940s, although her two most successful novels were published in the 1970s after a fifteen-year dry spell. In addition to writing fiction, Welty also established her importance as a critic with such works as *The Eye of the Story: Selected Essays and Reviews* (1978). Over her lifetime, she won numerous awards and honors and became a favorite college lecturer.

The Writer's Life

Eudora Alice Welty was born on April 13, 1909, in Jackson, Mississippi. She was the oldest of three children of Christian Webb Welty and Mary Chestina Andrews Welty. Both of her parents were newcomers to Jackson. Christian grew up on a farm in Ohio, while Chestina, as she was called, was reared in the mountains of West Virginia. They met one summer while Christian worked in West Virginia near where Chestina worked as a schoolteacher. They married in 1904 and selected the promising town of Jackson, Mississippi, as their home. The home on Pinehurst Street, to which the family moved while Welty was in high school, would become her lifelong residence.

Childhood. Reading was Welty's passion for as long as she could remember. As a child, she especially enjoyed myths and fairy tales. She was also a voracious reader, who read "everything that stood before [her]," as she noted in her memoir, *One Writer's Beginnings* (1984). When she was nine years old, her mother brought her to the local library to apply for her first library card.

Welty's closely knit family included her two younger brothers, Edward and Walter. The family took Sunday drives together in the family automobile, as well as summer driving trips to visit relatives in Ohio and West Virginia. Her father introduced Welty to photography, which would become a lifelong hobby.

College. After Welty graduated from Central High School in 1925, she enrolled at the Mississippi State College for Women in Columbus, where she began to write short stories and poems. In 1927 she transferred to the

Born in a house on North Congress Street, not far from the state capitol, Welty was a lifelong resident of Jackson, Mississippi, shown here in an undated photograph.

University of Wisconsin in Madison, where she majored in English. Upon graduating in 1929, the beginning of the Great Depression, she returned home for a year before entering a year-long graduate course in advertising at Columbia University Graduate School of Business in New York. Her beloved father died shortly after her return home to Jackson in 1931.

The Emerging Writer. Welty's first paying job was writing for a Jackson radio station. She also served as a society reporter for the *Memphis Commercial Appeal.* In 1935 she became a publicity agent for the Works Progress Administration (WPA) in Mississippi, for which she traveled throughout the state, taking photographs and interviewing people. She visited New York often, looking for jobs and trying to get her photos and short stories published.

Welty's first short story, "Death of a Traveling Salesman," was published in 1936 in *Manuscript.* The following year, the poet novelist and critic Robert Penn Warren accepted Welty's "A Piece of News" for *The Southern Review,* of which he was coeditor. "Petrified Man" appeared in *O. Henry Prize Stories* of 1939. That year, Welty met fellow southern writer Katherine Anne Porter, who became Welty's mentor and lifelong friend.

Welty around 1945. Her early experiences helped shape Welty's strong ear for dialogue and her sharp eye for nuance. Of her craft she has said, "What I do in the writing of any character is to try to enter into the mind, heart and skin of a human being who is not my-self. It is the act of a writer's imagination that I set the most high."

Breakthrough. By 1940, Welty had seen published only about one dozen short stories, mostly in regional quarterlies and small magazines. That year, however, she received a letter from Diarmuid Russell, who was interested in representing her as her literary agent. Welty would later credit Russell as the trusted counselor of her writing career, responsible for her break into the larger, and better-paying, literary markets. Also in 1940, Welty attended the Bread Loaf Writers' Conference in Middlebury, Vermont, where Porter was one of the speakers. The 1940s saw much more of Welty's work

published, beginning with two short stories that Russell sold to the *Atlantic Monthly,* one of the country's oldest and most prestigious magazines. Although magazines often balked at publishing her short stories, publishers expressed interest in her writing a novel. This proved problematic to Welty, who preferred the short story as the medium of choice to convey her unique vision. She believed that "novel" was synonymous with "plot," while she preferred the character development inherent in the short story. Welty prevailed and published her first collection of short stories, *A Curtain of Green and Other Stories,* in 1941, with an introduction by Katherine Anne Porter.

As she wrote her stories, however, Welty found that some became quite lengthy. One of these longer stories developed into her first

Among the shower of accolades Welty received during her lifetime was an honorary doctorate from her alma mater, the University of Wisconsin, in 1954.

novella, *The Robber Bridegroom,* published in 1942. In 1946, she succeeded in publishing her first full-length novel, *Delta Wedding,* which also began as a short story. She continued to submit stories for publication and published three more collections of new stories in later years.

Awards and Honors. Welty's story "A Worn Path" won second prize in the O. Henry Award competition in 1941. This was followed by two consecutive first place O. Henry Awards for "The Wide Net" in 1942 and for "Livvie" in 1943. She also won Guggenheim Fellowships in 1942 and 1949. In 1952 she was elected to membership in the National Institute of Arts and Letters. In 1954 she lectured at Cambridge University in England, received an honorary doctorate from the University of Wisconsin, and published her third novel, *The Ponder Heart,* which was adapted for the Broadway stage in 1956.

From 1955 to 1970, however, Welty wrote more than she published. In part, this may reflect personal problems. In 1956 her long-time agent and friend Diarmuid Russell suffered a heart attack. Then, in 1959, her brother Walter died after a long illness. He would be followed in 1966 by Welty's mother and her brother Edward, who died within four days of each other. This was also the last year in which Welty would publish a new short story. In the wake of these losses, however, she produced her two last and best-received novels. *Losing Battles,* published in 1970 and dedicated to her brothers, became her biggest seller and prompted some of her previous work to be reissued. Two years later, *The Optimist's Daughter* (1972) won the Pulitzer Prize. Throughout the 1980s and 1990s Welty was honored with various awards, including the Gold Medal of the National Institute of Arts and Letters (1972), the National Medal for Literature (1979), and the U.S. Medal of Freedom (1980). In 1987 she was made Chevalier de l'Ordre des Arts et des Lettres in France, and she was inducted into France's Légion d'Honneur at the Old Capitol building in Jackson in 1996.

College Lecturer. Because Welty could not live on her income as a writer until after the publication of *Losing Battles* and *The Optimist's Daughter* in the 1970s, she supplemented her income by visiting colleges and lecturing and reading her short stories. One series of lectures, which she delivered at Harvard University in 1983, won both the American Book Award and the National Book Critics Circle Award after it was published as *One Writer's Beginnings* (1984). By 1990, old age combined with an injury, arthritis, and hearing loss had marked the end of Welty's long and productive writing career, characterized by her agent as "a sustained struggle for deserved recognition."

HIGHLIGHTS IN WELTY'S LIFE

1909	Eudora Alice Welty is born April 13 in Jackson, Mississippi.
1925	Graduates from Central High School; enters the Mississippi State College for Women in Columbus.
1929	Completes bachelor's degree at the University of Wisconsin in Madison.
1930	Attends one-year advertising course at the Columbia University Graduate School of Business in New York City.
1931	Returns home to Jackson; father dies.
1935	Becomes publicity agent for Works Progress Administration (WPA).
1936	Publishes her first short story, "Death of a Traveling Salesman."
1939	Befriends fellow southern writer Katherine Anne Porter.
1940	Enlists Diarmuid Russell as literary agent.
1941	Publishes her first short-story collection, *A Curtain of Green and Other Stories*.
1942	Publishes her first novella, *The Robber Bridegroom;* wins first Guggenheim Fellowship.
1946	Publishes her first full-length novel, *Delta Wedding*.
1952	Elected to the National Institute of Arts and Letters.
1954	Lectures at Cambridge University in England.
1956	Attends New York opening of stage adaptation of her novel *The Ponder Heart*.
1959	Her brother Walter dies.
1966	Her mother and her brother Edward die.
1970	Welty publishes *Losing Battles*.
1972	Publishes *The Optimist's Daughter* which wins the Pulitzer Prize; receives Gold Medal of the National Institute of Arts and Letters.
1973	Her longtime friend and agent, Diarmuid Russell, dies.
1979	Welty wins National Medal for Literature.
1980	Receives the U.S. Medal of Freedom from President Jimmy Carter.
1984	Publishes *One Writer's Beginnings,* which wins the American Book Award and National Book Critics Circle Award.
1987	Made Chevalier de l'Ordre des Arts et des Lettres in France.
1996	Inducted into France's Légion d'Honneur at Old Capitol building in Jackson.
2001	Dies on July 23, in Jackson, Mississippi

The Writer's Work

Although Eudora Welty believed herself to be primarily a short story writer, some of her greatest success, both critically and financially, was achieved through her novels. She even won praise from fellow southerner William Faulkner for her first novella, *The Robber Bridegroom*. Both in her short stories and her novels, Welty usually focused on ceremonies or crises, such as weddings or funerals— occasions fraught with change and mixed emotions.

The Art of Storytelling. Welty was an avid observer and listener with a fantastic memory who was able to translate real-life experiences into compelling fiction. For Welty, born and bred in the South, storytelling was an integral part of life. Her fiction reflects distinctive aspects of the oral storytelling tradition. Welty favors action over description and uses simple sentences, colloquialisms, and colorful verbs. She has written that her narrative style was influenced by a friend of her mother, who told

One of Welty's great gifts was to imbue her characters with vitality and believability, while still preserving their quirkiness and dignity. Thomas Hart Benton's *Cotton Pickers, Georgia* (Metropolitan Museum of Art, New York) presents the type of scene that marked Welty's formative years and on which she heavily drew in her writing.

long, rambling tales of local gossip. Welty shaped this form of digressive monologue into an art. She also had the storyteller's knack for exaggerating certain details while excising others, all in order to make a good story. Her characters themselves illustrate this concept, defining themselves by the very stories they tell.

Yet Welty often parodies the southern art of storytelling. Small-town rural life often evokes the ideas of simplicity and leisure. Family and visiting are cherished concepts, and conversation is pleasurable and social. Rather than glorify storytelling as a social art, however, Welty's characters often talk because they have nothing better to do. Rural life is often portrayed as isolated and lonely. People gossip, sometimes in a very mean-spirited way, endlessly repeating the same stories to spice up their otherwise monotonous existence. Nevertheless, Welty shows compassion for even the humblest of characters.

Family Versus the Outsider. Family relationships are Welty's specialty. In fact, the family, with all its rituals and conventions, has long been considered a defining characteristic of southern culture, embodying the notions of devotion and unity. Welty's concept of family is, however, more complex, a source of both stability and love as well as of deep frustration. Welty exposes the imperfections that lie beneath the seeming normalcy of the traditional family. Although her families can be sources of hospitality, generosity, and kindness, they can also be small-minded, petty, and even hostile to nonmembers.

In contrast to the family unit is the figure of the outsider—an orphan, a traveler, or someone who has married into the family. Although initially welcomed, the outsider must eventually choose sides and either accept the family/community's values and become a part of the unit or forever remain apart, wandering, and rootless. In many of Welty's stories, the individual is seen to be a product of one's own family but is at the same time struggling to gain some measure of individuality. Family duty and obligation can conflict with one's own aspirations.

The Importance of Place. Welty believed that place was integral to a story and relied

Rural Mississippi emerges as a multilayered and very real backdrop, informing and shaping Welty's work. Otto Dix's 1921 oil painting *Woman with Child* suggests the figures Welty came across in her travels in her home state.

heavily on her rural Mississippi landscape—its scenery, its economy, and its inhabitants—as the setting for most of her fiction. She once wrote, "Every story would be another story, and unrecognizable as art, if it took up its characters and plot and happened somewhere else." Yet the Mississippi of Welty's fiction is uniquely hers, for she also believed that there were "as many ways of seeing a place as there are pairs of eyes to see it."

Welty used setting to help delineate her characters, believing that they needed to be placed against a backdrop that would confine and thus define them. Paradoxically, many of Welty's characters desire to be someplace other than where they are. Her characters usually make some kind of journey, whether physical or spiritual. There are also often wandering figures, such as traveling salesmen, circus performers, and other transients, who arrive in the setting to breathe fresh air into the residents' stale surroundings. Welty has written that she herself was fascinated by traveling artists, who frequently passed through Jackson on their way to New Orleans.

BIBLIOGRAPHY

Carson, Barbara Harrell. *Eudora Welty: Two Pictures at Once in Her Frame.* Troy, N.Y.: Whitston, 1992.

Devlin, Albert J., ed. *Welty: A Life in Literature.* Jackson: University Press of Mississippi, 1987.

Evans, Elizabeth. *Eudora Welty.* New York: Frederick Ungar, 1981.

Gretlund, Jan Nordby. *Eudora Welty's Aesthetics of Place.* Newark: University of Delaware Press, 1994.

Kreyling, Michael. *Author and Agent: Eudora Welty and Diarmuid Russell.* New York: Farrar, Straus and Giroux, 1991.

Manning, Carol S. *With Ears Opening Like Morning Glories: Eudora Welty and the Love of Storytelling.* Westport, Conn.: Greenwood Press, 1985.

Schmidt, Peter. *The Heart of the Story: Eudora Welty's Short Fiction.* Jackson: University Press of Mississippi, 1991.

Trouard, Dawn, ed. *Eudora Welty: Eye of the Storyteller.* Kent, Ohio: Kent State University Press, 1989.

Vande Kieft, Ruth M. *Eudora Welty.* New York: Twayne Publishers, 1962. Rev. ed. New York: Twayne Publishers, 1987.

Waldron, Ann. *Eudora: A Writer's Life.* New York: Doubleday, 1998.

NONFICTION

1948 Music from Spain
1949 The Reading and Writing of Short Stories
1957 Place in Fiction
1962 Three Papers on Fiction
1971 One Time, One Place: Mississippi in the Depression, a Snapshot Album
1974 A Pageant of Birds
1978 The Eye of the Story: Selected Essays and Reviews
1979 Ida M'Toy
1980 Miracles of Perception: The Art of Willa Cather (with Alfred Knopf and Yehudi Menuhin)
1984 One Writer's Beginnings
1985 In Black and White
1989 Eudora Welty: Photographs
1994 A Writer's Eye: Collected Book Reviews, ed. Pearl Amelia McHaney

1995 Eudora Welty, Other Places

SHORT FICTION

1941 A Curtain of Green and Other Stories
1943 The Wide Net and Other Stories
1949 The Golden Apples
1950 Short Stories
1954 Selected Stories of Eudora Welty
1955 The Bride of the Innisfallen and Other Stories
1980 The Collected Stories of Eudora Welty

LONG FICTION

1942 The Robber Bridegroom
1946 Delta Wedding
1954 The Ponder Heart
1970 Losing Battles
1972 The Optimist's Daughter

CHILDREN'S LITERATURE

1964 The Shoe Bird

EUDORA WELTY
The Robber Bridegroom

A HARVEST BOOK

One Writer's Beginnings

Genre: Autobiography
Subgenre: Instructional lecture
Published: 1984
Time period: 1909–1984
Setting: Mississippi

Themes and Issues. This glowing memoir of Eudora Welty's childhood was her last published original writing. Its reception by both critics and the general public was overwhelming. Not only did the book win both the American Book Award and National Book Critics Circle Award, but it also became an instant best-seller, appearing for forty-six weeks on the *New York Times* best-seller list.

When writer Ann Waldron asked Welty's permission to write her biography, she refused, saying "Your private life should be kept private." Undeterred, Waldron made several trips to Jackson to do research. When she would stop at Welty's home, the ever-gracious author invariably invited her in. Yet Waldron never obtained Welty's consent to write about her, and when Waldron published *Eudora: A Writer's Life* in 1998, the first-ever biography on Welty, it was unauthorized.

Although Welty guarded her privacy, she broke tradition when she delivered a series of three lectures at Harvard University in April 1983, which were published the following year as *One Writer's Beginnings*. In the lectures, Welty revealed much about her family background and childhood. As much as the memoir reveals about her early life, however, it falls short of a full account. It ends before her literary career actually began.

In her memoir, Welty writes, "Long before I wrote stories, I listened for stories." One of the key elements in Welty's work is her love of stories, not only those written in the books she avidly read, but also those told orally. Many of the tales Welty relates happened before she was born and were obviously passed on by her mother, Mary Chestina Andrews Welty, who was herself an avid storyteller.

The Plot. In one story, when Chestina, as she was called, was a girl, she once ran back into the family's burning home to rescue a beloved set of books by Charles Dickens. In another story, fifteen-year-old Chestina was charged with making the arduous journey with her ailing father in the dead of winter from her family's remote mountaintop home in West Virginia to a hospital in Baltimore. When her father died on the operating table, she brought the coffin back home to her mother and five younger brothers for burial.

It is striking that Welty's reminiscences about her mother's family consist of stories about people, reflecting her mother's role as storyteller, whereas her reminiscences about her father's family consist of descriptions of their house and its contents, which she remembered from visits. In truth, Welty never knew much about her father's family, because they were not storytellers. Nevertheless, Welty's father introduced her to photography, which perhaps helped develop her eye for detail and setting. She wrote that taking a photo captured a transient moment, and writing about it was her method of developing it.

These stories of family history are interspersed with Welty's own remembrances, many from her childhood, perhaps themselves influenced by the storyteller's art she inherited from her mother. Her fascination with the notion of the journey as a literary device stems from the summer road trips her family made. Welty's account of one trip, during which her father negotiated winding rural gravel roads, some of which petered out and forced him to back the car up for miles in its own dust, evokes Judge Moody's frustrating automobile trip in *Losing Battles* (1970).

In her fiction as in her memoir, Welty blends past and present events. Because she often veered from the traditional linear narrative form, critics claimed that her stories were "obscure" and "plotless." Her reasoning was that "The events in our lives happen in a sequence in time, but in their significance to ourselves they find their own order, a timetable not necessarily . . . chronological." One of the most striking examples of this mode in her fiction is found in *The Optimist's Daughter* (1972), in which the protagonist Laurel reflects continually on past events as she sits with her dying father, attends his funeral, and prepares to return to Chicago.

Analysis. Welty wrote that her greatest treasure, in both her life and her work, was her memory. However, she also believed in the importance of allowing memories to be flexible and open to reinterpretation. Through the flexibility of fiction, Welty was able to play with her own memories, developing them and redeveloping them in myriad ways, perhaps conveying truths about her own life that her genteel southern upbringing would not have allowed.

In this memoir one comes to understand the important role Welty's parents played in her life. They were by nature opposites: Christian was an optimist, Chestina a pessimist; Christian was a Yankee, Chestina a southerner. The happy marriage of Welty's parents inspired her fascination with paradoxes, which she would explore in her fiction. In addition, her parents' overprotectiveness only provoked her desire to exceed her boundaries, her thirst to know more. Her memoir ends on that note: "As you have seen, I am a writer who came of a shel-

One Writer's Beginnings emerged as a necessary look back on a long and fruitful life. Welty ends her brief account with three aptly summational sentences: "As you have seen, I am a writer who came of a sheltered life. A sheltered life can be a daring life as well. For all serious daring starts from within."

Alexander Deineka's *The Road to Mt. Vernaunt* reflects Welty's cherished childhood memories of long family drives. Welty describes herself as a child climbing into the back seat of the family car and commanding the other passengers, "Now talk!" As a writer, she privileged the value of listening. "Long before I wrote stories, I listened for stories. Listening for them is something more acute than listening to them. When their elders sit and begin, children are just waiting and hoping for one to come out, like a mouse from its hole."

tered life. A sheltered life can be a daring life as well. For all serious daring starts from within."

SOURCES FOR FURTHER STUDY

Carson, Barbara Harrell. "Confluence: *One Writer's Beginnings.*" In Eudora Welty: *Two Pictures at Once in Her Frame.* Troy, N.Y.: Whitston, 1992.

Mortimer, Gail L. *Daughter of the Swan: Love and Knowledge in Eudora Welty's Fiction.* Athens: University of Georgia Press, 1994.

Prenshaw, Peggy Whitman, ed. *Conversations with Eudora Welty.* Jackson: University Press of Mississippi, 1984.

Reader's Guide to Major Works

THE GOLDEN APPLES

Genre: Short story collection
Subgenre: Drama
Published: New York, 1949
Time period: 1900 to 1940s
Setting: A fictional Mississippi town

Themes and Issues. Eudora Welty's own favorite among her books, *The Golden Apples* was inspired by a poem by W. B. Yeats, "The Song of the Wandering Aengus." This theme of wandering is echoed in several of the main characters, who travel restlessly in a never-ending quest for love and knowledge, which often remain elusive. The stories share a cast of characters, all residents of the imaginary town of Morgana, Mississippi. The stories appear in chronological order, spanning some forty years, and depict the characters at various stages of their lives. Welty once said that the stories were "interrelated, but not inter-dependent."

The Plot. "Shower of Gold," the first story in the collection, introduces King MacLain, who in some way figures in all the stories. He is a traveling salesman and a notorious womanizer, thus a wanderer in both a geographical and an ethical sense. Although he marries and has twin boys, he is rarely at home.

The tragic second story, "June Recital," centers on the town's piano teacher, Miss Eckhart, an outsider of German origin who is never accepted by the town and eventually goes mad. "Sir Rabbit" recounts a sexual encounter between King and a young woman in the woods. A local girls' camp becomes the setting for "Moon Lake" for which Loch Morrison, a Boy Scout, is drafted to serve as the camp's lifeguard. He saves the life of an orphan girl, Easter, who accidentally falls into the lake. It is hinted that both of these children may actually be King's illegitimate offspring.

"The Whole World Knows" and "Music From Spain" center on King's twin boys as adults, one of whom has remained in Morgana, and the other of whom has moved to San Francisco. "Music From Spain" is the only story in the collection that is not set in Morgana. The final story, "The Wanderers," brings the collection full circle with the death and funeral of Virgie Rainey's mother, who was the narrator of the first story, set about forty years earlier.

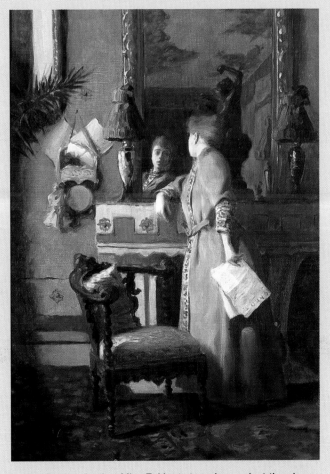

In *The Golden Apples*, Miss Eckhart struggles against the clannish residents of Morgana and the provincial way they view their community and her lack of inclusion in it. When, at the beginning of the book Welty lists the main families of the town, the Eckharts are not included. Miss Eckhart is an outsider and feels the constant sting of the resulting isolation, as suggested by Paul Chabas's oil painting *A Glance in the Mirror*.

Analysis. The theme of the wanderer figures throughout most of this collection, with King MacLain and Virgie Rainey as the two principal wanderers. King passes on his sense of wanderlust to his sons, one of whom even makes it as far as San Francisco. Virgie, a girl of ill repute from a poor family, in the end becomes one of the town's few successes. Miss Eckhart of "June Recital" is also a wanderer.

Of all Welty's characters, Miss Eckhart is the essence of Welty's own fictional voice. Welty wrote in *One Writer's Beginnings:* "What I have put into her is my passion for my own life work, my own art." Because of the small-mindedness of the town's residents, Miss Eckhart is never accepted as one of them. She, however, devotes herself to one of her students whom she feels is very talented, Virgie Rainey. Virgie does not appreciate Miss Eckhart's attentions. Over time, the townspeople stop sending their daughters for lessons, and Miss Eckhart moves away.

In "June Recital," while Virgie trysts with a sailor upstairs in the now-vacant MacLain house, where Miss Eckhart once lived and maintained her piano studio, scenes of a maddened Miss Eckhart returning to burn down the house are interspersed with the memories of one of her students, Cassie Morrison, of an elegant June recital Miss Eckhart gave years before. The cyclical nature of the stories reinforces the idea that life goes on, that one can still emerge triumphant despite, or perhaps because of, the surrounding community, much as Virgie Rainey does.

SOURCES FOR FURTHER STUDY

Gretlund, Jan Nordby. "The Morgana Community." In Eudora Welty's *Aesthetics of Place.* Newark: University of Delaware Press, 1994.

Gygax, Franziska. "*The Golden Apples:* Female Myths and the Woman Artist." In *Serious Daring from Within: Female Narrative Strategies in Eudora Welty's Novels.* New York: Greenwood Press, 1990.

Schmidt, Peter. "Misogyny and the Medusa's Gaze: Welty's Tragic Stories." In *The Heart of the Story: Eudora Welty's Short Fiction.* Jackson: University of Mississippi Press, 1991.

LOSING BATTLES

Genre: Novel
Subgenre: Comic epic
Published: New York, 1970
Time period: 1930s
Setting: Rural northeast Mississippi

Themes and Issues. When it appeared after Welty's nearly fifteen-year absence from publishing, *Losing Battles* more than made up for lost time. An uncharacteristically long work for Welty, the novel highlights some of her best literary qualities, most particularly her characterizations and her humor. *Losing Battles* is a deceptively complex tale told in a rambling, leisurely style mirroring the conversation and storytelling of the main characters.

The Plot. The story begins on the day of the family reunion of the extended Vaughn-Renfro-Beecham clan at the impoverished family homestead in the red clay hills of northeast Mississippi. The family is celebrating the ninetieth birthday of Granny Vaughn, who raised her granddaughter, Beulah, and six grandsons after the deaths of their parents. All but Beulah and Beulah's husband and children have moved away, so the bulk of the family has made the journey home for this momentous occasion. The family is also anticipating the heroic return of Beulah's nineteen-year-old son, Jack Renfro, who has been in jail.

The story unfolds slowly. Jack does indeed arrive and, in a curious twist of fate, helps a stranded motorist along the way who turns out to be the same judge who sent him to prison. Jack's family is offended to hear this, and they tell Jack he should go push Judge Moody's car right back into the ditch where he belongs. Because of the peculiarity of the local roads, Jack knows exactly where to find the judge. Thus begins a comic series of mishaps in which the judge's car once again goes off the road and becomes perched precariously on the edge of a precipice, from which Jack does his best to rescue it.

Analysis. In *Losing Battles,* Welty both tells a sprawling tale of the poor white farmers of

In *Losing Battles,* a family, such as the one portrayed in Honore D. Sharrer's *Tribute to the American Working People* (Smithsonian American Art Museum, Washington, D.C.), gathers in a show of force and unity. However, the high comedy of the novel masks the deep division that actually typifies the clan.

northeast Mississippi during the 1930s and pokes fun at the South and its values. Although the family is shown to embody the traditional values of love, honor, and devotion, the reality is quite different. Their apparent unity is a sham—most of them have scattered across the state and do not even correspond with each other. One member has been in prison, and another has murdered a man and allowed an innocent man to be punished for the crime. Although the family members are devoted to one another, especially to those who are deceased, they readily bad-mouth anyone else. Moreover, despite their apparent gregariousness, they appear to be completely ignorant of anything or anyone outside their small world.

The battles of the novel's title are many. Jack battled a local bully to protect his sister's honor and to retrieve a family heirloom only to lose and be sent to prison. Judge Moody has difficulty navigating the local roads and must battle not only to retrieve his car from its precarious perch but also to save it from Jack's sincere but bungling efforts to help. Another ironic quirk of fate has the judge and his wife attending Jack's family reunion while they are on their way to attend the funeral of a venerable local schoolteacher, Miss Julia Mortimer. Julia Mortimer herself fought a lifelong uphill battle against illiteracy only to watch her best students move away. Throughout, Welty parodies the South's ability to see victory in defeat, much as it did after the Civil War, and treats the human comedy with the sense of humor it deserves.

SOURCES FOR FURTHER STUDY

Carson, Barbara Harrell. "The Tie That Binds: Losing Battles." In *Eudora Welty: Two Pictures at Once in Her Frame.* Troy, N.Y.: Whitston, 1992.

Donaldson, Susan V. "'Contradictors, Interferers, and Prevaricators': Opposing Modes of Discourse in Eudora Welty's *Losing Battles.*" In *Eudora Welty: Eye of the Storyteller,* edited by Dawn Trouard. Kent, Ohio: Kent State University Press, 1989.

Manning, Carol S. "*Losing Battles:* Tall Tale and Comic Epic." In *With Ears Opening Like Morning Glories: Eudora Welty and the Love of Storytelling.* Westport, Conn.: Greenwood Press, 1985.

THE OPTIMIST'S DAUGHTER

Genre: Novel
Subgenre: Drama
Published: New York, 1972
Time period: 1960s
Setting: Mount Salus, Mississippi

Themes and Issues. Welty's last published novel appears to be an autobiographical work. Elements from Welty's own life are directly reflected: The protagonist returns home to accompany a parent to New Orleans for eye surgery, her personal ambitions conflict with her sense of familial obligation, and she is at her father's side when he dies.

The Plot. Forty-something widow Laurel McKelva Hand is called home to Mount Salus, Mississippi, from her job in Chicago in order to accompany her elderly father to New Orleans for eye surgery. Along for the ride is her father's new wife, Fay. Laurel's own mother, Becky, died years earlier. Laurel and Fay, although about the same age, are a study in contrasts. Where Laurel is quiet and introspective, Fay is chatty and shallow. It soon becomes apparent that the two women do not like each other. Laurel has long wondered, in fact, what her father sees in Fay.

Although Judge McKelva's surgery goes well, he dies while convalescing in the hospital. Laurel and Fay must then accompany the body back to Mount Salus and prepare for the funeral. Because the judge was a long-standing member of the community, his funeral is well attended. Most of the guests are friends and neighbors who knew both the judge, his first wife, and Laurel well. Fay, an outsider from Texas, was never a part of the Mount Salus community.

Fay is depicted as self-centered and selfish. During the funeral, she throws herself on the coffin of her dead husband, screaming that he had no right to die and leave her all alone, an act which mortifies Laurel. After much soul-searching, which climaxes in a last confrontation with Fay, Laurel returns to Chicago.

Analysis. This deceptively simple book is a departure from Welty's previous novels. Although not without humor, *The Optimist's Daughter* forgoes comedy for a serious and in-depth examination of a middle-aged woman in the throes of a midlife crisis.

Multiple conflicts emerge between Laurel and Fay, between the past and the present, and more broadly, between the Old South and the New South. Laurel and her father are of the genteel Old South, with its stately family homes, love of reading and books, and strong sense of tradition and community. Fay, the newcomer, resents all the neighbors who show up uninvited at "her" house to pay their respects. Fay is concerned only with herself and does not even invite her own family to the funeral.

The passing of Judge McKelva symbolizes the death of the Old South and its traditional ways. Laurel feels guilty that she left Mount Salus. Had she stayed with her father after her mother died, he might not have married Fay. Fay, who inherits the family home, points the direction of the New South. She is ignorant of the old ways and proud of it. She and her mother even discuss turning the stately home into a boardinghouse.

After reflecting extensively on her past, Laurel is finally able to understand that the optimism she inherited from her father comes less from their ability to see the bright side of life than from their refusal to face its dark side. As Laurel begins to see things from Fay's point of view—that Fay's theatrics at the funeral were her way of maintaining her own family's traditions, that Fay felt isolated amid her husband's disapproving family and friends—Laurel gains

In *The Optimist's Daughter,* Fay, an emblem of grasping and crass individualism, divides the remaining members of the McKelva family, similar to the central figure in Hyacinth Manning-Carner's 1954 painting *Fragmented.*

SOME INSPIRATIONS BEHIND WELTY'S WORK

Over the course of her lifetime, Eudora Welty resisted attempts by biographers to chronicle her life, insisting that "your private life should be kept private." She preferred to be judged by her fiction. Nevertheless, it is clearly evident that aspects of her life heavily influenced her fiction.

The fact that Welty never married and lived at home with her mother for most of her life might explain why several of her strongest and most memorable characters were spinsters, such as the schoolteacher Miss Julia Mortimer of *Losing Battles* and piano teacher Miss Eckhart of *The Golden Apples* (1949).

Welty's mother was herself a storyteller. Welty learned much about her mother's family through the stories her mother told her. In contrast, she knew much less about her father's side of the family. Welty sometimes was taken to visit the mountaintop home of her mother's family in rural West Virginia, where she met her grandmother and her five left-handed banjo-playing uncles, the inspiration for her 1970 novel, *Losing Battles*. Her mother's eye surgery surely influenced her award-winning 1972 novel, *The Optimist's Daughter.*

It is interesting to note that whereas her hometown of Jackson figures prominently in her memoirs, Welty rarely set stories in Jackson itself. Nevertheless, the state of Mississippi is the setting of most of her short stories and novels. Welty's position as a publicist for the Works Progress Administration in the 1930s allowed her the opportunity to travel widely throughout the state of Mississippi. In the course of her travels she met a variety of people and photographed many different regions. The vast wealth of information she accumulated undoubtedly enriched her fiction. Although Welty was a native Mississippian, she had lived in Wisconsin and New York and thus had attained the outsider's detachment and viewpoint. This alternate point of view sometimes put her in the position of the outsider, a theme that would appear often in her fiction.

Welty's photographs for the Works Progress Administration (WPA), such as "Blind Weaver," documented the everyday lives of Mississippians. Of the form, Welty has written, "Photography taught me that to be able to capture transience, by being ready to click the shutter at the crucial moment, was the greatest need I had."

compassion. Furthermore, this compassionate insight helps Lauren learn to let go of her need to see only the positive aspects of her parents and her past, and she then is able to leave Mount Salus and return to Chicago.

SOURCES FOR FURTHER STUDY

Gretlund, Jan Nordby, and Karl-Heinz Westarp, eds. *The Late Novels of Eudora Welty.* Columbia: University of South Carolina Press, 1998.

Kreyling, Michael. "The Culminating Moment: *To the Lighthouse* and *The Optimist's Daughter.*" In *Eudora Welty's Achievement of Order.* Baton Rouge: Louisiana State University Press, 1980.

Manning, Carol S. "*The Optimist's Daughter:* Rewriting the Southern Novel." *In With Ears Opening Like Morning Glories: Eudora Welty and the Love of Storytelling.* Westport, Conn.: Greenwood Press, 1985.

Other Works

"DEATH OF A TRAVELING SALESMAN" (1936).

The first story that Eudora Welty published maps out territory to which she would return repeatedly. The plot centers on the last day in the life of a traveling salesman, R. J. Bowman. As he drives through rural Mississippi, he lands his car in a ravine and seeks help from a pair of nearby farm people.

Sonny and his pregnant wife, unlike many of Welty's later characters, are markedly taciturn. As the story unfolds, their disinclination to waste words becomes symbolic of their physical poverty. When it gets dark, Sonny must go "borry some fire" from a neighbor. This line, which Welty heard from a neighbor who heard it while in the country, was so evocative that she created an entire story around it.

Bowman has spent his career on the road. A recent illness temporarily stopped his travels and forced him, as he lay idling in bed, to reflect on his peripatetic existence. The young couple symbolize a spiritual richness that shows up the poverty of his own lonely materialistic existence. Unfortunately, Bowman comes to this realization too late. He dies of a heart attack alone on the road, before making it back to his car.

Of her story, Welty has said, "As usual, I began writing from a distance, but 'Death of a Traveling Salesman' led me closer. It drew me toward what was at the center of it. . . . 'A marriage, a fruitful marriage. That simple thing.' Writing 'Death of a Traveling Salesman' opened my eyes. And I had received the shock of having touched, for the first time, on my real subject: human relationships."

"PETRIFIED MAN" (1939). This short story, first published in the *Southern Review,* also appeared in *O. Henry Prize Stories of 1939.* Ironically, Welty had burned the first draft because it had been rejected by so many magazines. When Robert Penn Warren decided to reconsider it, Welty had to rewrite the story from memory.

"Petrified Man" is a humorous tale set in a small-town beauty shop and centers on two appointments, a week apart, of Mrs. Fletcher to have her usual shampoo-and-set by the very voluble Leota. Leota keeps up a running conversation, feeding Mrs. Fletcher all the local gossip.

The plot, such as it is, centers on Leota's recent friendship with a Mrs. Pike from New Orleans. During the first appointment, Leota is very upbeat, happy with her new acquaintance. By the second appointment, Leota is noticeably upset, making Mrs. Fletcher's head sore with her overzealous scrubbing.

Throughout, Leota comes across as another of Welty's eccentric small-town women. Although shallow and a gossip, Leota is also basically good-hearted. The title refers to a performer in a traveling freak show, who turns out to be a serial rapist. Leota is piqued because it was Mrs. Pike who recognized him and turned him in, collecting a sizable reward, which she does not share with Leota.

"WHY I LIVE AT THE P.O." (1941). One of her most popular stories stemmed from a glimpse Welty had of an ironing board open in a country post office. It is an excellent example of a Welty "monologue that takes possession of the narrator."

Told in the first person, this tragicomic tale centers on a young woman named Sister who lives at home with her mother, grandfather, and uncle. The return of her sister, Stella-Rondo, who has separated from her husband, provokes old jealousies. As it is the Fourth of July, fireworks fly both at home and outside.

Sister, in a fit of pique, snatches up her belongings and heads for the post office, of which she is postmistress.

Sister's complaints about the favoritism shown Stella-Rondo may be justified. Sister not only works at a job outside the home but also appears to do most of the work around the house. By taking the family's radio, among other items, and moving into the post office, Sister effectively cuts the family off from the outside world. The pettiness of her plight, however, is made clear as she gloats to news of World War II playing on the radio in the background.

"A WORN PATH" (1941). "A Worn Path" was one of the first of Welty's stories to be published in the *Atlantic Monthly,* and it won second prize in the O. Henry Award competition in 1941. Unlike most of Welty's fiction, this story centers on an elderly black woman. Although Welty mentions African Americans, few figure as characters in their own right, indicative of racial separation in Mississippi at the time Welty was growing up there.

Phoenix Jackson makes regular trips on foot from her remote home in the hills to the town of Natchez to get medicine for her young grandson, who swallowed lye when he was a toddler. She seems an unlikely choice for such a journey, but there are only the two of them left. Their interdependence is the thing that gives meaning to their lives.

The poignancy of the woman's journey is heightened by the fact that it is Christmastime. The image of the town's residents carting prettily wrapped packages amid red and green electric lights contrasts sharply with the lonely old woman, her hair tied in a red rag, her apron made of bleached sugar sacks. In the end, one questions whether the boy is even still alive, or whether she makes the journey from sheer force of habit.

Anne Goldthwaite's undated watercolor *The Coiffeur* captures the main action around which "Petrified Man" centers. The stylist Leota emerges as a woman with a good heart, but prey to her own petty jealousies and sharp tongue.

Resources

Most of Eudora Welty's manuscripts, photographs, and correspondence are located in Jackson at the Mississippi Department of Archives and History. A comprehensive guide to the collection *The Welty Collection: A Guide to the Eudora Welty Manuscripts and Documents at the Mississippi Department of Archives and History* (1988) has been prepared by Suzanne Marrs and published by the University Press of Mississippi. Other sources of interest to students of Eudora Welty include the following:

Eudora Welty Newsletter. The twice-yearly newsletter was established in 1977 as a source of scholarship and information about the life and work of Eudora Welty. The newsletter's Web site features a brief biography, a selected bibliography, and lists of books about Welty and her work and honors and awards she received, as well as recent news and notes in Welty scholarship. (http://www.gsu.edu/~wwwewn/)

The Mississippi Writers Page, Eudora Welty. The Mississippi Writers Page, a Web site sponsored by the University of Mississippi English Department, features a page devoted to Eudora Welty, with a substantial article on Welty's life and work, as well as related information and links. (http://www.olemiss.edu/depts/english/ms-writers/dir/welty_eudora/)

Audio Recordings. Many recordings have been made of Welty and others reading and discussing her work, including *The Optimist's Daughter* (1999) from Random House Audiobooks, *Eudora Welty Reads: Why I Live at the P.O., Powerhouse, Petrified Man and Other of Her Stories* (1998) from Caedmon, and *Eudora Welty on Story Telling* (1961) from Jeffrey Norton.

Interview. Welty was interviewed by Roger Mudd on the PBS television news program *The MacNeil/Lehrer Newshour* on November 29, 1989, show number 3613.

C. K. BRECKENRIDGE

Edith Wharton

BORN: January 24, 1862, New York, New York

DIED: August 11, 1937, St.-Brice-sous-Forêt, France

IDENTIFICATION: Early-twentieth-century novelist known for her vivid depictions of life in New York's post–Civil War and turn-of-the-century high society.

Edith Wharton achieved her greatest literary success with stories of late–nineteenth-century New York's fashionable society. Her novels *The House of Mirth* (1905) and *The Age of Innocence* (1920) portray the social and moral complexities of life in the New York of her youth, a society of old money, new ambition, and rigid hierarchies whose conventions demanded strict conformity. Wharton's ability to capture the details of everyday life as well as the larger issues of individual freedom and social responsibility won her a wide readership and critical acclaim. In 1921 Wharton received the first Pulitzer Prize in fiction awarded to a woman, and her books have continued to attract interest among modern readers.

The Writer's Life

Edith Wharton was born Edith Newbold Jones, the youngest of three children, on January 24, 1862. Her father, George Fredric Jones, was a gentleman of leisure with ties to some of the oldest families in New York. Her mother, Lucretia Stevens Rhinelander Jones, was also descended from early New York settlers. The family occupied a handsome brownstone near Fifth Avenue and Madison Square Park. Wharton's father derived his wealth from land holdings in Manhattan, and the family was highly placed in the tightly knit New York society that later formed the basis for some of Wharton's most celebrated novels.

Childhood. In 1866 Wharton's father moved the family to Europe as U.S. currency began to depreciate because of a post–Civil War economic recession. Wharton spent six years living in France and Italy and traveling in Spain and Germany. While visiting Germany's Black Forest region in 1870, she fell ill with typhoid fever and nearly died. For several years afterward, she suffered from attacks of extreme fear.

Education. The family returned to New York in 1872, and Wharton began her studies under the guidance of Anna Bahlman, a nineteen-year-old German girl who had served as governess to the daughters of a family friend. Anna was expected to prepare Wharton for her entrance into society as a woman of good breeding and impeccable manners who would not fail to attract a suitable husband.

During her years in Europe, Wharton learned French and Italian, and she began studying German. She was drawn to the world of books at an early age and began making up stories to entertain herself. While holding open books she could not yet read and pacing up and down hallways, she composed stories and recited them as they came to her. In her father's library, she devoured books of English and French literature, art history and criticism, philosophy, and architecture. Wharton's excessive bookishness troubled her mother and strained the relationship between them.

Aspiring Author. Wharton cherished her father's library as a haven where she could read and think. She began to compose stories and verse, even publishing in a New York newspaper a poem that she had submitted at the age of thirteen in what she called "a moment

Edith Wharton in her early twenties, peers from the staircase in her home.

of unheard of audacity." Two years later, she published a group of poems in the prestigious *Atlantic Monthly*. A friend of her brother had shown the poems to Henry Wadsworth Longfellow, who offered his endorsement. Wharton completed a book of poems, which her mother published privately under the title *Verses* (1878), and a novel called *Fast and Loose* (1977), which was never published in her lifetime.

Social Debut and a Return to Europe.

Amid growing concerns over her devotion to books and desire to write, Wharton's parents decided to celebrate her debut in New York society at the age of seventeen, a year earlier than expected. Shortly afterward, her father's declining health, also a possible factor in her early debut, prompted the Jones family to return to Europe in 1880.

Wharton traveled to Italy with her family in 1881. Her travels in Europe, and particularly in Italy, made a lasting impression on her artistic sense. Wharton loved the ancient villas and gardens, and she discovered what she called "a background of beauty and old-established order" that would remain with her for the rest of her life. In the spring of 1882, her father was stricken with paralysis and died in Cannes, France. Although her relationship with her parents was often aloof, Wharton had found in her father a companion who shared her love of beautiful things and who understood, more than any other family member, the creative impulses that moved her.

Courtship and Marriage.

Upon their return from Europe in 1882, Wharton and her mother moved to a smaller house at West Twenty-fifth Street and Fifth Avenue. She became engaged to Harry Stevens, a prominent figure in New York society; Harry's mother opposed the marriage, however, and the engage-

Wharton was a woman who capitalized on the advantages her privileged life offered. Her worldliness and vast education allowed her to cast a critical eye on the inner workings of her upper-class society.

ment was broken. In 1883 Edith fell in love with Walter Berry, a young lawyer and distant cousin. Although he did not return her affection, they remained intimate friends until his death in 1927.

Later in 1883, Wharton began seeing Edward Wharton, a friend of her brother Harry. Thirteen years her senior, Edward was good-humored and shared with her a love of animals and travel. They were married on April 29, 1885, and moved into a small cottage on the grounds of Pencraig, an estate in Newport, Rhode Island.

Domestic and Creative Life.

Wharton and her husband, whom she called Teddy, spent the early years of their marriage renovating the cottage house in Newport and traveling several months each year in Europe. Wharton began to write again, publishing three poems and meeting Edward Burlingame of *Scribner's* magazine, in which many of her novels would later be serialized. Burlingame became her lifelong friend and literary advisor.

In the years between 1890 and 1900, Wharton began to make a name for herself as an author, publishing her first short story, "Mrs. Manstey's View" in 1890; a book on interior design written in collaboration with the architect Ogden Codman, Jr., called *The Decoration of Houses* in 1897; her first collection of short stories, entitled *The Greater Inclination*, in 1899; and a novella, *The Touchstone*, in 1900. Codman helped the Whartons renovate their first home, Land's End, in Newport, and would remain a close friend throughout Wharton's life.

Wharton's other works included *Crucial Instances* (1901) and her first novel, *The Valley of Decision* (1902), a period piece set in eighteenth-century Italy. Wharton enjoyed a growing reputation as a writer, and her works were selling well. She began friendships with the French novelist Paul Bourget and the American expatriate Henry James, who lived in England. Both men remained lifelong friends and confidants. Through this period, Wharton began to see herself as an author and gained confidence in her writing ability.

In 1902, following the death of Wharton's mother and a sizable inheritance, the Whartons moved into their new home, the Mount, in Lenox, Massachusetts. It was a large house, built with the assistance of Ogden Codman, Jr., with sprawling gardens designed by Wharton herself. Life in the

Edith and Teddy had been married for little more than ten years when this photograph of him was taken in 1896.

country and the comfort of a luxurious home and surrounding gardens agreed with the couple, and Wharton settled in to the life of a writer.

Creative and Personal Conflicts. Wharton secured her literary legacy with the publication of *The House of Mirth* in 1905, her first novel to chronicle the social and moral climate of the New York of her youth. The book was a bestseller and brought her international recognition.

As Wharton's literary success grew, however, her personal life began to suffer. She struggled with bouts of depression and frequent illness,

HIGHLIGHTS IN WHARTON'S LIFE

1862   Edith Wharton is born Edith Newbold Jones on January 24 in New York City.

1866   The Jones family moves to Europe to economize.

1877   Wharton writes a novel entitled *Fast and Loose*, unpublished until 1977.

1878   Wharton's mother arranges a private printing of Wharton's *Verses*.

1880   Wharton travels in Europe with her parents; father dies in Cannes, France.

1885   Marries Edward Wharton on April 29 in New York City.

1890   Publishes her first short story, "Mrs. Manstey's View."

1897   Publishes *The Decoration of Houses* with Ogden Codman, Jr.

1899   *The Greater Inclination*, Wharton's first collection of short stories, is published.

1901   Begins building the Mount in Lenox, Massachusetts.

1902   Publishes her first full-length novel, *The Valley of Decision*.

1903   Begins friendship with novelist Henry James.

1905   Publishes *The House of Mirth*, her first novel set in old New York, which becomes a best-seller.

1907   Rents a second home in Paris; visits Europe more frequently; begins three-year affair with the journalist Morton Fullerton.

1913   Divorces Edward Wharton.

1914   Organizes refugee work in France during World War I; is awarded the Legion of Honor medal in 1916.

1920   Publishes *The Age of Innocence*, for which she receives a Pulitzer Prize the following year.

1923   Returns to United States to receive an honorary doctorate from Yale University.

1934   Publishes an autobiography, *A Backward Glance*.

1937   Dies at Pavillon Colombe in St.-Brice-sous-Forêt, France, on August 11.

1938   Her unfinished last novel, *The Buccaneers*, is published posthumously.

and her relationship with Teddy became more remote. She spent longer periods of time each year in Europe, and Teddy too began to show symptoms of mental instability. Depressed and inexplicably elated in turns, Teddy complained of imaginary ailments. His financial and marital infidelities and Wharton's own passionate affair with the American journalist Morton Fullerton hastened the end of their marriage. After several years of struggling with their emotional and intellectual differences, the Whartons divorced in 1913.

The War. The outbreak of World War I in Europe in 1914 brought new struggles for Wharton, who had been living almost exclusively in Europe since 1909. Wharton organized relief efforts for refugee families from Belgium and France and established workhouses for French women whose husbands had gone to fight. She also carried food and medical supplies to the front lines. For her service to France during World War I, the French government awarded her the Legion of Honor medal in 1916.

After witnessing the horrors of war at first hand and suffering the loss of several close friends, including the novelist Henry James in 1916, Wharton turned her attention once again to her youth in New York. She published *The Age of Innocence* in 1920. Perhaps the crowning achievement of her literary career, it earned her a Pulitzer Prize in 1921. Two years later, she made her last visit to the United States, to receive an honorary degree from Yale University, another first for a woman.

The Last Years. After becoming comfortably settled in Pavillon Colombe, an eighteenth-century house in the village of St.-Brice-sous-Forêt north of Paris that she purchased in 1919, Wharton continued to write. She published eight more novels and an autobiography in the years between 1922 and 1934. She also indulged her passion for gardening, a diversion she

had not enjoyed since her years at the Mount in Lenox, Massachusetts.

In 1935 Wharton suffered a stroke that left her temporarily sightless in one eye. Although she recovered, her health remained poor. Early in 1937 she suffered a second stroke that immobilized her. She died on August 11, 1937, at Pavillon Colombe and was buried in the Cimetière des Gourds at Versailles, next to her dearest friend, Walter Berry.

By the time she was in her early forties, Wharton had cemented her place in American letters with the publication of *The House of Mirth*.

The Writer's Work

Edith Wharton wrote in many different genres, producing short and long fiction, nonfiction, poetry, and plays, most of which were stage adaptations of her own works. Her literary reputation, however, rests largely on her novels, particularly those that chronicle life in late-nineteenth-century New York. These novels exhibit Wharton's keen understanding of the social and moral currents within New York's social hierarchies and an eye for the smallest details of day-to-day life. All her writing, whether fictional or otherwise, evokes a strong sense of the people and places she describes. It realistically portrays the inner and outer lives of her characters.

Issues in Wharton's Fiction. In 1905 Wharton published *The House of Mirth*, the first of several novels set in the New York society of her youth. The extravagant lifestyles of New York's idle rich seemed to her at first too superficial and dull to interest readers. She concluded, however, that "a frivolous society can acquire dramatic significance only through what its frivolity destroys. Its tragic implication lies in its power of debasing people and ideals." This frivolous society, ruled by complex but ultimately superficial class distinctions and conventions, becomes the background against which creative and dynamic individuals struggle for life. Wharton's best books capture these struggles in vivid and tragic detail.

Wharton was able to present that world with clarity and realism because she herself had felt its restrictive and debasing qualities. She observed the social rituals, the personalities, and the moral failings of New York's fashionable set as a young woman and later as a married society matron. She witnessed the changes brought on by the rise of post–Civil War millionaire in-

FILMS BASED ON WHARTON'S STORIES

1918 *The House of Mirth*

1923 *The Glimpses of the Moon*

1924 *The Age of Innocence*

1929 *The Marriage Playground*

1934 *The Age of Innocence*

1935 *Strange Wives*

1939 *The Old Maid*

1960 *Ethan Frome* (TV)

1981 *Summer* (TV)

1981 *The House of Mirth* (TV)

1993 *Ethan Frome*

1993 *The Age of Innocence*

1995 *The Buccaneers* (TV)

1997 *The Reef* (released in U.S. as *Passion's Way*, 1999)

2000 *The House of Mirth*

In the 1880s, New York City's Fifth Avenue had become the fashionable address for the city's rich. Considered by some to be an insulated world of disproportionate wealth, Wharton was able to use her ivory tower to observe and skewer the folly and frivolity of those around her.

dustrialists, who used their newfound wealth as capital for social acceptance in the closely knit aristocracy of New York. She also suffered within the narrowly defined roles, both socially and intellectually, that women were compelled to accept.

People in Wharton's Fiction. Wharton's fiction depicts a broad range of characters, from the austere bastions of Old World conventions, Mr. and Mrs. Henry van der Luyden, and the irreverent but respectable Mrs. Manson Mingott in *The Age of Innocence* to the newly moneyed social climber and millionaire Simon Rosedale and the altruistic Gerty Farrish in *The House of Mirth*. Wharton's capacity to create realistic characters of all social classes adds a necessary balance to her depictions of their social and moral struggles.

Some of Wharton's most intriguing and psy-chologically complex characters include Lily Bart, the beautiful but penniless socialite in *The House of Mirth*, the long-suffering New England farmer Ethan Frome in the novella of the same name, the sensitive and passionate Anna Leath in *The Reef* (1912), the thwarted lovers Newland Archer and Ellen Olenska in *The Age of Innocence*, and the calculating Christiane de Treymes in *Madame de Treymes* (1907).

The Theme of Entrapment. Many of Wharton's characters feel trapped by relationships and social conventions that stifle their personal development. Any expression of creativity and passion would put them at odds with society, so they often must weigh their future happiness against that of others. The dynamic of self-expression and self-denial and the need to maintain personal integrity while also remaining a part of a social whole adds depth to Wharton's characters and substance to their moral conflicts. The theme of entrapment often manifests in social or romantic triangles where individuals' creative or emotional needs draw them away from conventional or repressive relationships.

Stage and Screen. Although Wharton did not write for the stage, many of her works were adapted for production by her and others. She also received substantial royalties for the purchase of film rights to many of her novels and short stories. Her first book to be adapted for the stage was *The House of Mirth*, which debuted at the Savoy Theater in New York in 1906. The production was a failure with critics and audiences alike.

In 1928, however, a production of *The Age of Innocence* enjoyed a successful run in New York and made a four-month tour of nine other cities. Wharton's greatest success on the stage occurred with the production of *The Old Maid* in 1935. Dramatized by the poet, novelist, screenwriter, and playwright Zoë Akins, it won a Pulitzer Prize for drama and continued its run for the next two years.

Wharton's Literary Legacy. Wharton's success as an author peaked between 1905 and 1920. *The House of Mirth*, published in 1905, established her as a major American writer, and *Ethan Frome*, which appeared in 1911, was regularly taught in schools during her lifetime. Wharton's extraordinary range of nonfiction work, including books on architecture, interior design, and several volumes documenting her travels in Europe and beyond, reveals her versatility as a writer and a scholar.

Wharton's legacy as an author is secure despite the decline in both readership and critical

Wharton borrowed heavily from the text of her own life. Hers was the story of an independent woman trying to assert herself within the often restrictive confines and rigid codes of upper-class society.

SOME INSPIRATIONS BEHIND WHARTON'S WORK

Although Edith Wharton's family largely ignored her interest in literature and her success as a writer, Wharton acknowledged that her parents' insistence on speaking correct English helped shape her elegant writing style. Her parents' greatest contribution to Wharton's future success as a writer, however, was the large family library, in which she first became acquainted with the masterpieces of literature.

Wharton's travels in Europe as a child and young adult also influenced her future writing. She possessed a remarkable visual memory of the places she visited and the details of interior and exterior design. Her ability to re-create these scenes added a realism and vitality to her work.

As an internationally best-selling author, Wharton made many friends in the American and European literary world. Perhaps the most influential of her contemporary writers was Henry James, with whom she maintained a close friendship from 1900 until his death in 1916. Critics note that some of Wharton's works are similar in both style and structure to those of James. Among all her many friends, both literary and otherwise, no one was closer than Walter Berry. Wharton relied on him for literary advice and personal support, and upon her death she was buried in a cemetery plot next to his.

A still from the film version of *The Age of Innocence*, starring Daniel Day-Lewis as Newland Archer and Michelle Pfeiffer as Ellen Olenska. The need to please society and a hypocritical sense of morality conspire to stifle true love.

acclaim of her later works, such as *The Glimpses of the Moon* (1922), *Twilight Sleep* (1927), and *The Children* (1928). Wharton helped to inspire the next generation of American novelists, including Sinclair Lewis and F. Scott Fitzgerald. Her novels and short stories remain compelling to modern readers and enjoy a prominent place in school and university curricula.

BIBLIOGRAPHY

Ammons, Elizabeth. *Edith Wharton's Argument with America*. Athens: University of Georgia Press, 1980.

Benstock, Shari. *Edith Wharton: No Gifts from Chance*. New York: Charles Scribner's Sons, 1994.

Bloom, Harold, ed. *Edith Wharton*. New York: Chelsea House, 1986.

Dwight, Eleanor. *Edith Wharton: An Extraordinary Life*. New York: Harry N. Abrams, 1994.

Kellog, Grace. *The Two Lives of Edith Wharton*. New York: Appleton-Century, 1965.

Lewis, R. W. B. *Edith Wharton*. New York: Harper & Row, 1975.

Lewis, R. W. B., and Nancy Lewis, eds. *The Letters of Edith Wharton*. New York: Macmillan, 1988.

Lindberg, Gary H. *Edith Wharton and the Novel of Manners*. Charlottesville: University Press of Virginia, 1975.

Wharton, Edith. *A Backward Glance*. New York: Charles Scribner's Sons, 1964.

Wolff, Cynthia Griffin. *A Feast of Words*. New York: Oxford University Press, 1977.

Reader's Guide to Major Works

THE AGE OF INNOCENCE

Genre: Novel
Subgenre: Social satire
Published: New York, 1920
Time period: 1870s
Setting: New York City

Themes and Issues. In the emotionally cold and intellectually dull environs of New York's polite society, Edith Wharton examines issues of personal freedom and social obligation, of passion and responsibility. Through the eyes of Newland Archer and Ellen Olenska, Wharton contrasts the desires these characters hope to satisfy with the traditions by which they ultimately choose to live. Considered by many critics to be her finest work of fiction, this novel was conceived in the last years of World War I, during which so much of Wharton's own world had changed. Her description and dramatization of the near-forgotten era of old New York illustrate what is gained and what is potentially lost in the acceptance of a social system and the values required of the individuals within it.

The Plot. Newland Archer is engaged to the beautiful but unimaginative May Welland. A product of her surroundings, May has been trained to be attractive, entertaining, and predictable. Newland enjoys the comfort of old New York's social routines but feels superior to its polished surface and superficial values. He anticipates that May will blossom under his care and become the woman he envisions as his ideal intellectual and emotional partner.

Into Newland's comfortable world enters the intriguing and exotic Ellen Olenska, a distant cousin of May's and a former member of New York society who has returned to her family to escape her disastrous marriage to a Polish nobleman. At once, Newland is drawn to Ellen's independence no less than to her beauty. Although the rest of New York is scandalized by Ellen's presence in polite society and by the rumors attending the circumstances of her flight from her husband, Newland becomes her advocate. He convinces Mr. and Mrs. Henry van der Luyden, the final arbiters of good taste and breeding in New York, to extend their support to the unfortunate Ellen.

Newland is commissioned by Ellen's family to advise her in divorce proceedings against

Coiffed and on display, a young woman waits apprehensively on the edges of *The Ball,* a painting completed around 1878 by James Jacques Joseph Tissot (Musée d'Orsay, Paris). In *The Age of Innocence,* Wharton suggests that society is a performance and its rules a construction that often stands as an obstacle to happiness and self-fulfillment.

her husband. Perhaps predictably, the two fall in love. Newland is fascinated by Ellen's resistance to the petty taboos of polite society and her freedom of thought. He considers breaking his engagement to May and marrying Ellen. The family, sensing his intentions, contrives to keep Newland and Ellen apart. As Ellen's presence in New York grows increasingly intolerable to her family, many members of which have retracted their previous acceptance of her, Ellen decides to leave for Europe. Although Newland is now married to May, he considers following Ellen; however, when May announces that she is pregnant, Newland realizes that he is finally trapped.

Many years later, Newland and his son visit Paris. May is dead, and Newland's children are grown, while Ellen is a widow living alone. Newland's son has made an appointment for them to see Ellen, but Newland gets only as far as a bench outside her apartment. He sends his son in to see her while he remains outside, preferring the memory of his past relationship with Ellen to the possibility of resuming it.

Analysis. Wharton's portrayal of New York society in *The Age of Innocence* is less severe than its characterization in *The House of Mirth*, written fifteen years earlier. Similar situations exist in both these works. Polite New York society remains narrow and repressive, its values seem shallow and their adherents hypocritical, and the individual seeking freedom must always confront an unfeeling and code-driven collective. The difference, however, is one of perspective. The choices that Newland and Ellen feel compelled to make are essentially good ones: honoring personal and family obligations to avoid causing others pain.

The House of Mirth's Lily Bart, however, must choose between a materially comfortable but morally bankrupt life within society and the

LONG FICTION

1900	The Touchstone
1902	The Valley of Decision
1903	Sanctuary
1905	The House of Mirth
1907	Madame de Treymes
1907	The Fruit of the Tree
1911	Ethan Frome
1912	The Reef
1913	The Custom of the Country
1917	Summer
1918	The Marne
1920	The Age of Innocence
1922	The Glimpses of the Moon
1923	A Son at the Front
1924	Old New York
1925	The Mother's Recompense
1927	Twilight Sleep
1928	The Children
1929	Hudson River Bracketed
1932	The Gods Arrive
1938	The Buccaneers
1977	Fast and Loose

SHORT FICTION

1899	The Greater Inclination
1901	Crucial Instances
1904	The Descent of Man
1908	The Hermit and the Wild Woman
1910	Tales of Men and Ghosts
1916	Xingu and Other Stories
1926	Here and Beyond
1930	Certain People
1933	Human Nature
1936	The World Over
1937	Ghosts
1968	The Collected Short Stories of Edith Wharton

POETRY

1878	Verses
1909	Artemis to Actæon
1926	Twelve Poems

NONFICTION

1897	The Decoration of Houses (with Ogden Codman, Jr.)
1904	Italian Villas and Their Gardens
1905	Italian Backgrounds
1908	A Motor-Flight Through France
1915	Fighting France from Dunkerque to Belfort
1919	French Ways and Their Meanings
1920	In Morocco
1925	The Writing of Fiction
1934	A Backward Glance
1988	The Letters of Edith Wharton
1991	The Cruise of the Vanadis
1997	The Uncollected Critical Writings, Frederick Wegener, ed.

hardships required of those who live on its fringes. Although society in *The House of Mirth* conspires to protect its baser aspects, the same society in *The Age of Innocence* conspires to preserve its virtues. This contrast reflects perhaps a change in Wharton's feelings at a time when she was better able to view the society of her own painful adolescence and young adult life in a more sympathetic light.

SOURCES FOR FURTHER STUDY

Bell, Millicent, ed. *The Cambridge Companion to Edith Wharton.* New York: Cambridge University Press, 1995.

Colquitt, Clare, Susan Goodman, and Candace Waid, eds. *A Forward Glance: New Essays on Edith Wharton.* Newark: University of Delaware Press, 1999.

Singley, Carol, ed. *"The Age of Innocence": Complete Text with Introduction, Historical Contexts, and Criticism.* New York: Mariner Books, 2000.

Waid, Candice, ed. *"The Age of Innocence": Authoritative Texts, Contexts, and Criticism.* New York: Norton, 2000.

ETHAN FROME

Genre: Novella
Subgenre: Tragic drama
Published: New York, 1911
Time period: Early 1900s
Setting: Isolated Massachusetts village

Themes and Issues. Wharton uses the desolate winter landscape of a rural Massachusetts village to portray the physical and emotional

The wintry setting is essential to Wharton's *Ethan Frome.* The bleak and lifeless landscape, suggested here by Claude Monet's *Ice Floes on the Seine at Bougival* (Musée D'Orsay, Paris), mirrors the cold emotional distance that grows between the characters.

suffering of Ethan Frome through the eyes of a shadowy, unnamed narrator. By framing the story of Ethan's life with the narrator's personal observations of present events and his vision of Ethan's past, Wharton makes the narrator a significant focal point of the book and the act of telling Ethan's story becomes as important as the events being related.

Death is an important theme in the story, but not necessarily physical death. No character in this story dies. The isolated and barren landscape of Starkfield, implied by its very name and reflected in Ethan's dilapidated and cold farmhouse, suggests an opposition of outer suffering and inner hopelessness, a life that mirrors the grave.

The Plot. An engineer, the narrator of this story, arrives in Starkfield during the winter on a work assignment and hires Ethan Frome to drive him each day to the train station, where he commutes to his job. The engineer previously has witnessed Ethan's daily trips to the post office, and he has inquired about his history among the townspeople. He finds Ethan, although burdened with disabilities and a "ruin of a man," a striking person.

The two men return from the train station one evening during a heavy snowstorm, and Ethan suggests that they both spend the night at his farmhouse. As they approach the front door, the narrator hears a voice within; the story then moves from the present to the past, as the narrator offers a "vision" of Ethan's story. This vision describes Ethan's hard life on a failing farm, his marriage to Zenobia, a disagreeable older woman, and his budding affection for Zenobia's destitute cousin, Mattie Silver, who lives with the Fromes as a housekeeper.

Zenobia, or Zeena, has suspicions about Ethan and Mattie's relationship and decides to hire a new housekeeper and send Mattie away. Unable to contradict his wife's wishes, Ethan submits and drives Mattie to the train station. On the way, he and Mattie stop to sled down a dangerous hill. They decide after climbing back up that they cannot part. Mattie convinces Ethan to make one more run down the

hill, this time aiming for a large elm tree and certain death. They plunge down the hill, but at the last moment Ethan sees a vision of his wife's face, and the sled veers away from the tree.

At this point the narrator's vision ends. The narrator is back at the threshold of Ethan's front door. As he enters, he sees Zeena, who now takes care of the severely injured Mattie, and Mattie, who is now a whining and disagreeable woman resembling Zeena's former self. The story ends with a conversation between the narrator and Mrs. Hale, the woman with whom he stays while in Starkfield. They agree that, though everyone in Ethan's household has suffered greatly, Ethan has suffered the most. Mrs. Hale notes that very little difference exists between the Fromes living in the farmhouse and the Fromes buried in the family graveyard.

Analysis. Wharton employs an unusual narrative technique in her telling of Ethan Frome's bleak history. Cynthia Griffin Wolff, in her article "Ethan Frome: 'This Vision of His Story,'" writes that "the 'story' of Ethan Frome is nothing more than a dream vision, a brief glimpse into the most appalling recesses of the narrator's mind." In this view, the story becomes "a terrified expression of the narrator's latent self—his alter ego."

Ethan Frome, then, can be understood in part as a story about storytelling. Ethan's cold and empty life, mirrored by the frozen New England landscape, also serves as a warning that emotional and intellectual repression, frequent themes in the story, can create an icy inner world of muted expression and unspeakable despair.

SOURCES FOR FURTHER STUDY

Lauer, Kristin O., and Cynthia Griffin Wolff, eds. *"Ethan Frome": Authoritative Text, Backgrounds, Contexts, and Criticism.* New York: Norton, 1995.

Smith, Christopher. *Readings on "Ethan Frome."* New York: Greenhaven Press, 2000.

Springer, Marlene. *"Ethan Frome": A Nightmare of Need.* New York: Twayne Publishers, 1993.

THE HOUSE OF MIRTH

Genre: Novel
Subgenre: Social criticism
Published: New York, 1905
Time period: 1890s
Setting: New York City

Themes and Issues. The New York of Wharton's youth was in transition from a society founded on inherited wealth and values to one based on unrestrained commercialism. After the Civil War, the rise of industrialism brought rapid and unimagined wealth to many outside New York's tightly knit social aristocracy. The invasion of new money created a breach in age-old traditions of respectability as the old social order was forced to make room for the new.

Within such a world, Lily Bart finds herself trapped. In a society of unrestrained speculation, represented by the influence of Wall Street, social interactions take on the nature of business transactions, as indicated by what one critic identifies as the prevalence in this novel of "the language of the marketplace." Lily is useful to society only if she confers value upon it. She is, then, at the mercy of a system whose shifting rate of exchange determines her fate.

The Plot. The bankruptcy and subsequent death of her father has left Lily Bart penniless. After the death of her mother, Lily lives with an aunt who provides her with minimal financial support and a begrudging hospitality. She realizes that she must marry into wealth but is unwilling to apply herself toward that end. She

Dewey Bates's painting *Daydreaming* evokes the solitude of Lily, pushed to the edges of society after a series of unforeseen setbacks.

begins to lose her social respectability, first among the old New York families and then with the newly rich industrialists.

Lawrence Selden, a casual acquaintance who becomes an increasingly intimate friend throughout Lily's mounting difficulties, has only a modest income. He is unwilling to propose marriage, though he and Lily love each other, because he cannot provide the luxuries that she desires. Meanwhile, Lily's position in society worsens after she incurs a financial obligation with Gus Trenor, who seeks an affair with her to satisfy the debt. Later, as the guest of Bertha Dorset, Lily travels to Europe on the Dorsets' yacht. She discovers Bertha's affair with a younger man, and Bertha, thinking that her husband is pursuing an affair with Lily, humiliates her by kicking her off the yacht before it leaves Europe.

Lily returns home to find that her aunt, from whom she had expected a large inheritance, has died and left her only a modest sum. She is forced to support herself by mending hats in a factory, but she has no talent for the job and is soon released. Penniless and without any social resources, she has two possible avenues that could improve her situation. The first is blackmail, a packet of correspondence between Selden and Bertha Dorset, with whom he had an affair. She is unwilling, however, to damage Selden's reputation in order to regain her social standing.

Finally, she receives the payment of ten thousand dollars as an inheritance from her aunt. She immediately pays her outstanding bills and returns the money she owes to Gus Trenor. Once more penniless and desperately ill, she dies from an accidental overdose of sleeping medicine.

Analysis. Wharton's aim in charting Lily's social and physical decline was to illustrate how a hedonistic and hypocritical society destroys those members who are unwilling or unable to accept its values. Lily has numerous opportunities to secure a wealthy husband, to manipulate and deceive in order to achieve social and financial independence. Although she is a victim of the cruel maneuverings of a selfish and unsympathetic society, she is also an agent of her own downfall. Like so many of Wharton's characters, Lily suffers all the more at the hands of a cold and cruel society because her own moral principles prevent her from responding in kind, even though doing so would potentially save her.

SOURCES FOR FURTHER STUDY

Bell, Millicent. *The Cambridge Companion to Edith Wharton.* New York: Cambridge University Press, 1995.

Dimock, Wai Chee. "Debasing Exchange." In *Edith Wharton's "The House of Mirth,"* edited by Shari Benstock. New York: St. Martin's, 1993.

Wolff, Cynthia Griffin. "Lily Bart and the Drama of Femininity." *American Literary History* 6, no. 1 (1994): 71–87.

Other Works

THE REEF (1912). In this novella, George Darrow, an international diplomat, and Anna Leath, an old friend and widow of a French nobleman, are about to be married. When Anna discovers that George has had an affair with her daughter's governess, Sophie Viner, who is also her stepson's fiancé, she must decide whether to abandon George, as her social upbringing demands, or to honor her own desires and marry him.

Anna faces a dilemma. If she marries George, she must break with the social traditions that have shaped her life thus far. If she parts with him, she must abandon the passionate awakening that their relationship has provided her. This novel owes much of its dramatic effect to the influence of Henry James. The unity between the story and its setting, a French château that reflects, in Edith Wharton's vivid descriptions of its features, the

A watercolor of Edith Wharton's chateau in France by Robert Norton. A master of setting and space, in *The Reef,* Wharton subtly illustrates the ways a house reflects the moods and temperaments of the people who inhabit it.

shifting emotions of its inhabitants, and the dramatic developments conveyed in turn through the consciousness of the principal players, all resemble techniques found in James's best works.

SUMMER (1917). In this novella, set in the small Massachusetts village of North Dormer, Charity Royall meets a visiting architect, Lucius Harney, and the two begin a passionate affair. When Lucius returns to his home in Boston, Charity discovers that she is pregnant and that Lucius is engaged to another woman. Her guardian, Lawyer Royall, who has previously proposed marriage, again renews his proposal. Faced with the shame of giving birth to an illegitimate child and unwilling to terminate the pregnancy, Charity accepts Lawyer's proposal and submits to a passionless though respectable marriage.

Charity's situation becomes more complex in light of her own origins as an illegitimate child from the poor mountain village above North Dormer. Her decision to ensure a proper future for her child at the expense of her own emotional needs is comparable with Ethan's reluctance, in Wharton's novella *Ethan Frome*, to leave his wife, although he finds his life with her intolerable.

Summer and *Ethan Frome* are viewed as companion stories because of the connections and differences among their main characters. Ethan's inability to articulate clearly his passion for Mattie and his disdain for Zeena shapes his life into an emotionally frigid and passive existence. Charity, who both articulates and indulges her passion, escapes Ethan's fate. Her decision to marry Lawyer, though unsatisfying emotionally, is a more mature response, and her awareness of a growing respect for Lawyer after her marriage seems to confirm the rightness of her decision.

Resources

Major collections of Edith Wharton's manuscripts can be found at Yale University's Beinecke Rare Book and Manuscript Library, the Harry Ransom Humanities Research Center at the University of Texas at Austin, and the Lilly Library at Indiana University. Other sources of interest to students of Edith Wharton include the following:

Edith Wharton Society. Founded by Professor Annette Zilversmit, the society publishes the *Edith Wharton Review* twice a year and maintains a useful Web site with links to electronic texts of Wharton's works. (http://www.ganzaga.edu/faculty/campbell/wharton)

Edith Wharton Restoration at the Mount. An organization in Lenox, Massachusetts, dedicated to the restoration and preservation of Wharton's home, the Mount, as well as the establishment of an educational center to promote Wharton studies.

Information about the organization and about Wharton's life can be found on its Web site. (http://www.edithwharton.org)

National Women's Hall of Fame. Located in the Women's Rights National Historical Park in Seneca Falls, New York, this organization was founded in 1969 to honor the contributions of American women. Its Web site contains a link to information on Edith Wharton's life. (http://greatwomen.org/whrtn.htm)

Edith Wharton's World: Portraits of People and Places. An on-line exhibit at the Smithsonian Institution Web site features biographical information on Wharton's life and portraits of people and places that were significant to her life and work. (http://www.npg.si.edu/exh/wharton)

PHILIP BADER

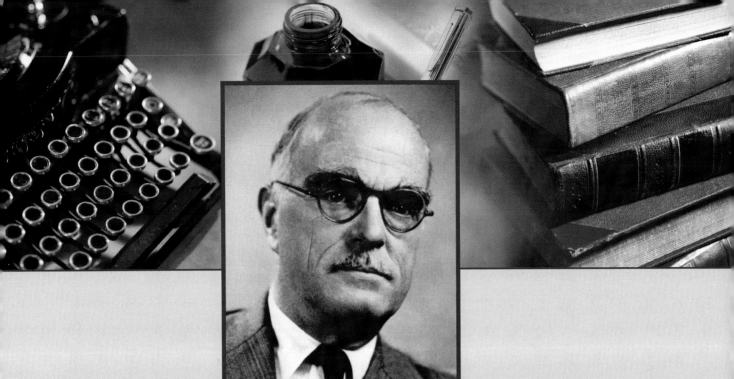

Thornton Wilder

BORN: April 17, 1897, Madison, Wisconsin
DIED: December 7, 1975, Hamden, Connecticut
IDENTIFICATION: Early twentieth-century playwright and novelist whose works were popular successes, although his full critical success was not achieved in his lifetime.

Although Thornton Wilder published his first play in 1920 and his first novel in 1926, he did not receive much critical attention until the extraordinary success of his second novel, *The Bridge of San Luis Rey* (1928), which was awarded a Pulitzer Prize. Because his works were more optimistic than the darker visions of his contemporaries, few critics considered Wilder a serious writer. However, Wilder is noteworthy for his modernist-influenced exploration of time and tradition and for his experimentation with minimalist staging techniques and semi-narrative forms. Two of his plays, *Our Town* (1938) and *The Skin of Our Teeth* (1942), were awarded Pulitzer Prizes, and with *The Matchmaker* (1954), continue to be among the most often produced American plays.

The Writer's Life

Thornton Niven Wilder was born on April 17, 1897, in Madison, Wisconsin, the second son of Amos Parker Wilder, editor of the *Wisconsin State Journal*, and his wife, Isabella Thornton Niven Wilder. Amos Wilder's political support of President Theodore Roosevelt led to a diplomatic appointment, which took the Wilders to Hong Kong in 1906, where Wilder attended a German-language school. While the family traversed the Pacific throughout the next several years, Wilder attended various schools in California and China, finishing with four years at Berkeley High School in California, from which he graduated in 1915.

College Years. After studying for two years at Oberlin College in Ohio, where he published his earliest prose and dramatic works, Wilder transferred to Yale University. World War I affected Wilder's studies; during the summer of 1918 he worked for the War Industries Board in Washington, D.C. He was turned down by all branches of the service because of his poor eyesight but was finally accepted by the Coast Artillery in 1919 and served for eight months at Fort Adams, Rhode Island. Upon his return to Yale, he joined the editorial staff of the *Yale Literary Magazine*, which published his first full-length play, *The Trumpet Shall Sound*, in 1920.

Wilder received his bachelor's degree from Yale in 1920 and continued his education in Rome, Italy, taking courses in archaeology from the American Academy. He returned to the United States to teach French at the Lawrenceville School in New Jersey, taking a leave of absence in 1924 to pursue graduate study in French literature at Princeton University. He received a master's degree from Princeton in 1925.

Recognition and Acclaim. In the following year, 1926, Wilder published his first novel,

The Wilder family on a Hong Kong street in a photograph from 1906. Amos, Wilder's father, was a U.S. consul general to Hong Kong and Shanghai. Thornton Wilder is standing next to his mother.

Wilder in a photo taken at the Lawrenceville School, where he taught French and was a master of Davis House. He took a leave of absence from the post to study at nearby Princeton, where he got the idea for his Pulitzer Prize–winning novel, *The Bridge of San Luis Rey*, "on the winding walk from the golf club to the Graduate College." He began to write the novel in his rooms on the top floor of the Graduate College and finished it in Davis House upon returning to Lawrenceville the following year.

FILMS BASED ON WILDER'S WRITING

1929	*The Bridge of San Luis Rey*
1940	*Our Town*
1944	*The Bridge of San Luis Rey*
1955	*The Skin of Our Teeth* (TV)
1955	*Our Town*
1958	*The Matchmaker*
1958	*The Bridge of San Luis Rey* (TV)
1969	*Hello, Dolly!*
1977	*Our Town*
1983	*The Skin of Our Teeth* (TV)
1988	*Mr. North*
1989	*Our Town* (TV)
1991	*Shadow of a Doubt* (TV)

The Cabala, and his first play, *The Trumpet Shall Sound*, was produced at the American Laboratory Theatre in New York under the direction of Richard Boleslavsky. Neither event was much noticed by critics or the public. In 1927, however, Wilder published his second novel, *The Bridge of San Luis Rey*, which became an immediate best-seller and won the Pulitzer Prize, which ensured Wilder's fame and the exuberant admiration of critics.

Wilder increased his popularity, if not his critical reputation, with the publication of two more novels, *The Woman of Andros* (1930) and *Heaven's My Destination* (1934), and a volume of one-act plays, *The Long Christmas Dinner and Other Plays in One Act* (1931) His adaptations of André Obey's *Le Viol de Lucrèce* (1932) for

Katharine Cornell and Henrik Ibsen's *A Doll's House* (1937) for Ruth Gordon placed his talents before the leading American directors and actors of the 1930s.

Further Success. In 1938 Wilder published *Our Town*, which won him his second Pulitzer Prize and would become his most-produced work. Neither the popularity of *Our Town* nor the Pulitzer Prize it earned impressed critics, who remained skeptical. In the same year Wilder completed *The Merchant of Yonkers*, an adaptation of Johann Nestroy's Austrian comedy *Einen Jux will er sich machen* that Wilder Americanized without losing the original's strength of plot. Wilder's play would later become better known as *The Matchmaker* (1954) and later still as the musical adaptation *Hello, Dolly!* (1964). *The Merchant of Yonkers* demon-

strated the skills at adaptation that Wilder had developed in the 1930s. Nevertheless, the play was a popular and critical flop.

Wilder had sufficiently impressed Alfred Hitchcock, however, that the British director, now working in Hollywood, sought him out to write a screenplay for his film *Shadow of a Doubt* (1943). Wilder accepted the job, although the war interrupted his writing, and it was ultimately completed by two other screenwriters. His next play, *The Skin of Our Teeth* (1942) seemed capable of winning back Wilder's audience and critics. It was loved by theatergoers and won Wilder a third Pulitzer Prize, but it also brought a spurious charge of plagiarism in a series of articles by the writers Henry M. Robinson and Joseph Campbell, accusing Wilder of plagiarizing *The Skin of Our Teeth* from James Joyce's novel *Finnegans Wake* (1939). Although he was soon vindicated by subsequent critics, Wilder seemed incapable of drawing serious positive criticism.

Success in Europe. While his plays continued to be produced in the United States, Wilder attracted new audiences in Great Britain with an American-cast production of *Our Town* (1946), an Edinburgh debut of *The Matchmaker* (1954), which simultaneously opened in London and New York the following year; *A Life in the Sun* (commonly known as *The Alcestiad*, 1956) at Edinburgh; and an American production in Paris of *The Skin of Our Teeth* (1956) sponsored by the U.S. State Department. In 1959 a French-language version of *The Matchmaker* was produced in Brussels, and a German-language version of *The Alcestiad* was staged in Zurich. An operatic version of *The Long Christmas Dinner* appeared in Mannheim, Germany (1961), and another German production of *The Alcestiad* in Frankfurt (1962).

Honors at Home. Wilder's European recognition was not overlooked by the Kennedy administration. President John F. Kennedy sponsored "An Evening with Thornton Wilder" for his cabinet and special invited guests on

By the time this photograph was taken, in the early 1940s, Wilder had already won two Pulitzer Prizes in a five-year span, thereby securing his reputation as an innovator of the American theater.

April 30, 1962. The following year Wilder was awarded the Presidential Medal of Freedom for his contributions to American culture. In 1965 he received the National Medal of Literature from President Lyndon B. Johnson. Now approaching his seventies, Wilder was looked upon as an artist summing up his career, and his last two novels reflected that attitude, whether or not Wilder shared it. *The Eighth Day* (1967), which won a National Book Award, took a cosmic viewpoint, seeing human history as only the latest moment in God's creation; the work after the seventh day of rest was not all complete. A similar optimism, between the lines of tragedy, could be seen in Wilder's final novel, *Theophilus North* (1973). With his last novel still selling well in the bookstores after two years, Wilder died of a heart attack on December 7, 1975, in Hamden, Connecticut, at the age of seventy-eight.

President Lyndon B. Johnson (at the podium) presents Wilder with the Presidential Medal of Freedom in the White House's State Dining Room on December 6, 1963.

HIGHLIGHTS IN WILDER'S LIFE

1897 Thornton Niven Wilder is born on April 17 in Madison, Wisconsin.

1906 Moves with family to Hong Kong, China, where father is American Consul General.

1909 Moves to Shanghai when father is transferred.

1915 Graduates from Berkeley High School; enrolls at Oberlin College in Ohio.

1917 Transfers to Yale University in New Haven, Connecticut.

1919 Serves with Coast Artillery at Fort Adams, Rhode Island, during World War I.

1920 Receives bachelor's degree from Yale; begins teaching French at Lawrenceville School, New Jersey.

1925 Receives master's degree in French literature from Princeton University.

1926 Publishes novel *The Cabala*; his play *The Trumpet Shall Sound* is produced in New York.

1927 Publishes novel *The Bridge of San Luis Rey*, which wins Pulitzer Prize.

1938 His plays *Our Town* and *The Merchant of Yonkers* are produced; *Our Town* wins Pulitzer Prize.

1942 Wilder writes screenplay for Alfred Hitchcock's *Shadow of a Doubt*; his play *The Skin of Our Teeth* is produced and wins Pulitzer Prize.

1950 Holds Norton Professorship of Poetry at Harvard University.

1954 Revises *The Merchant of Yonkers* as *The Matchmaker*.

1955 His play *A Life in the Sun* is produced.

1961 His opera *The Long Christmas Dinner* is produced.

1962 His three one-act plays, collectively known as *Plays for Bleecker Street*, are produced.

1963 Wilder receives Presidential Medal of Freedom.

1964 *Hello Dolly!*, a musical version of *The Matchmaker*, is produced.

1965 Wilder receives National Medal of Literature.

1967 Publishes novel *The Eighth Day*, which wins National Book Award.

1973 Publishes novel *Theophilus North*.

1975 Dies on December 7 in Hamden, Connecticut.

thornton wilder
Winner of the Pulitzer Prize

OuR ToWN

The Writer's Work

As an artist, Thornton Wilder presents a series of paradoxes. A disciple of the new humanism dedicated to preserving classical tradition, he pioneered new dramatic techniques that shattered tradition. Quintessentially American and modern, his early works were set in foreign countries and long ago. Faulted by some critics for appealing to mass audiences, Wilder was equally faulted, sometimes by the same critics, for ignoring the plight of common men and women.

Wilder's Americanism. Modernist writer Gertrude Stein, whom Wilder met in 1935, called the writers of her and Wilder's era "the lost generation," the alienated American writers between two world wars. These writers, such as Ernest Hemingway, F. Scott Fitzgerald, Eugene O'Neill, and Stein herself, repudiated what they felt were the narrow, Calvinist, restrictive values of the United States. They embraced, by becoming expatriates in Paris, what they felt were the more open, liberating, artistic values of Europe. Wilder, too, came to Paris in the years between the wars, but not, like his fellow writers, as an exile. He never denied his congregationalist Calvinism, and though he

Although Wilder's settings were often quintessentially American, his early works, such as his first novel, *The Cabala*, dealt with Americans in foreign lands. In *The Cabala* an American bumbles his way through Rome, the setting of Francois Marius Granet's 1808 painting *Trinita dei Monti and Villa Medici, Rome* (Louvre, Paris).

gained much from European exposure, he seemed to know instinctively that his strength came from his American identity.

Nevertheless, Wilder's early works of his lost generation years were not set in the United States and did not seem related to American concerns. *The Cabala* takes place in modern Rome, *The Bridge of San Luis Rey* in early eighteenth-century Peru, and *The Woman of Andros* in pre-Christian Greece. In all three novels, however, implicit parallels to modern American situations are apparent. All three deal with characters who are questioning the moral traditions being handed to them by an older culture.

The Cabala features an American character who sounds much like the disillusioned writers of the lost generation. In *The Bridge of San Luis Rey*, set sixty years before the American Revolution, there are no American characters. Yet the problems and sensibilities of the Peruvians in the novel all reflect the cultural inferiority complex of a New World colony in the face of its European mother country. *The Woman of Andros* pits the moralistic provincial island of Brynos against the supposedly more genteel and cultured Andros. Thus, all three novels ultimately echo the cultural situation of Wilder's America even though they are set in different places and eras.

Wilder's Optimism. Another quality that sets Wilder apart from his contemporary writers is his notorious optimism. The hallmark of the lost generation writers is their sense of alienation from their cultural tradition. For

Actors Frank Craven (the Stage Manager), Martha Scott (Emily Webb), and John Craven (George Gibbs) perform a scene from *Our Town*, Wilder's Pulitzer Prize–winning play, at the Morosco Theater in New York City in 1938.

these writers, classical (Greco-Roman) and Judeo-Christian worldviews no longer made sense of the world. Indeed, the new orthodoxy of modernism was that the world in fact does not make sense, for sense, or rational coherence, is a product of the human mind, not a part of nature. In the terms of the modernist philosophers, the world is absurd.

Wilder has been accused of ignoring this basic change in Western philosophy, but a close look at his work reveals that a loss of coherence in worldview is a vital theme in virtually every one of his plays and novels. In *The Bridge of San Luis Rey* the Peruvians, especially one Franciscan priest, attempt to make sense of a random catastrophe. In *Our Town* George and Emily try to make sense of that most irrational phenomenon, human love. In *The Skin of Our Teeth*, the Antrobus family faces a world falling apart and tries to hold their piece of it together.

Thus, while admitting with the other modernists that a former coherence was being lost, Wilder refused to agree with them that it might not, with a bit of a struggle, be recovered. It is Wilder's conviction that an order could be found that constitutes his optimism.

Stylistic Techniques. In addition to using modernist themes, Wilder also pushed the boundaries of form and style, experimenting in several novelistic and dramatic techniques. Both in his novels and on the stage Wilder chose a plot structure which Aristotle, and virtually all subsequent Western theorists, rejected

SOME INSPIRATIONS BEHIND WILDER'S WORK

Because Thornton Wilder wrote in the context of a literary movement that was a reaction to realism, most of his literary influences are writers of his generation or those whose major works appeared only a few years before his own. He learned from Henry James to present a psychological reality, rather than an empirical, scientific reality. He also shares with James the theme of the American abroad learning from an older European culture. In the fiction of James, the American invariably sheds his New World provincialism in favor of an Old World cosmopolitanism. In Wilder's fiction, however, the American may have his eyes opened to new possibilities, but he continues to value what is good in his own American culture.

The most visible influence on Wilder's dramatic revolt against realism is August Strindberg, who strove to present, especially in works such as *Ett drömspel* (1902; *A Dream Play*, 1912) and *Spöksonaten* (1907; *The Ghost Sonata*, 1916), not the external events of a person's life, but the felt, psychological impressions of a person's mental experience. Wilder's earliest plays, the apprentice works of his college days collected in *The Angel That Troubled the Waters and Other Plays* (1928), show this internalization of stage action, and his mature drama continues to develop the technique.

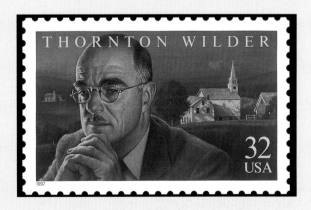

Thornton Wilder joined the Postal Service's literary arts series on the one-hundredth anniversary of his birth. The thirty-two-cent stamp was issued on April 17, 1997, in Hamden, Connecticut, where he lived at the end of his life.

Wilder had an abiding love of the theater—not only for dramatic structure but for the actors who embodied his rich and lively characters. Here he converses with Joanne Woodward and Paul Newman on October 3, 1959, at Circle-in-the-Square Theater in New York City. On that evening excerpts were performed from past productions, including Wilder's *Our Town*, in which Wilder himself assumed the role of the Stage Manager.

as inferior: the type of plot Aristotle called "episodic." The episodic plot is one in which one scene is not the logical development of the previous scene. Scenes are not causally connected in Wilder's drama and fiction, as Aristotle said they should be. In many ways this is the expected result of the absurdist worldview of modernism: Things simply happen.

Two experimental dramatic techniques that Wilder employed in his plays were minimalist staging and the revival of what the ancient Greeks called *parabasis*, a direct address of the audience. Wilder employed the first technique—eliminating props, sets, and curtain in order to focus on character and plot—early in his stage career, beginning with his one-act *The Long Christmas Dinner* and continuing with *Our Town*. He developed the second technique, *parabasis*, in his later works. In *The Matchmaker* Vandergelder addresses his philosophy to the audience, and the waiter who slips Cornelius his employer's purse justifies his action to the audience.

BIBLIOGRAPHY

Blank, Martin. *Critical Essays on Thornton Wilder*. New York: G. K. Hall, 1996.

Bryer, Jackson R. *Conversations with Thornton Wilder*. Jackson: University Press of Mississippi, 1992.

Burbank, Rex J. *Thornton Wilder*. 2d ed. Boston: Twayne Publishers, 1978.

Goldstone, Richard. *Thornton Wilder: An Intimate Portrait*. New York: Dutton, 1975.

Grebanier, Bernard. *Thornton Wilder*. Minneapolis: University of Minnesota Press, 1964.

Haberman, Donald. *The Plays of Thornton Wilder*. Middletown, Conn.: Wesleyan University Press, 1967.

Lifton, Paul. *"Vast Encyclopedia": The Theatre of Thornton Wilder*. Westport, Conn.: Greenwood Press, 1995.

McCasland, Elizabeth Barron. *The Philosophy of Thornton Wilder*. New York: Carlton Press, 1976.

Simon, Linda. *Thornton Wilder: His World*. Garden City, N.Y.: Doubleday, 1979.

Walsh, Claudette. *Thornton Wilder: A Reference Guide, 1926–1990*. New York: G. K. Hall, 1993.

Thornton Wilder and Shadow of a Doubt

Because Thornton Wilder's work on the screenplay of Alfred Hitchcock's *Shadow of a Doubt* was cut short by his military service and because he was adapting a story not his own, some fruitful parallels in character and theme between the film and his better-known work is often missed. Yet much of Wilder's best work is adapted from that of other writers, and the very fact that Hitchcock thought of Wilder after reading Gordon McDonnell's story and seeing *Our Town* suggests that Hitchcock saw in it some parallels to Wilder's work. Wilder initially thought the story contrived and joined the project only because of the money involved. Although he only spent five weeks on the screenplay before it was completed by other writers, he nevertheless left enough of a personal stamp on the film that comparison with *Our Town* and *Skin of Our Teeth* can be insightful.

The Wisdom of Adolescence. The most Wilderian element of the film is one of its biggest assets: the charming complexity of its main character, Charlotte Newton, or Young Charlie. She represents an eternal type Wilder explored both in Emily Webb of *Our Town* and in Gladys Antrobus of *The Skin of Our Teeth*. She is the adolescent girl who, in striving too hard to grow up, catches a glimpse of an eternal truth.

Young Charlie's first speech is also the one closest in theme and rhythm to those of Emily in *Our Town*. Although still in her teens, Charlie is already disillusioned with life. She laments the seemingly meaningless repetitions of daily routine and longs for a miracle to break her family out of its rut. She unwittingly echoes the world-weariness of her uncle, after whom she was named. Yet the elder Charlie's world-weariness results from his dissolute, criminal life. The excitement that Young Charlie hopes the elder will bring to their family is an excitement of evil and danger.

At first glance, this situation would seem to have nothing to do with that of *Our Town*. Emily does not find her day-to-day existence in Grover's Corners to be humdrum. In fact, she finds it just the opposite: She fears that her boyfriend, George, will go off to college and come to think that her small-town life, which is just fine with her, is too petty. It is precisely the mundane, in its simple everyday detail, that Wilder wants to capture.

Our Town's third act places the mundane in a different perspective—not one of evil and danger, as in *Shadow of a Doubt*, but one of death. A return to relive

Young Charlie Newton played by actress Teresa Wright, searches the eyes of her beloved Uncle Charlie, played by actor Joseph Cotten, in the 1943 motion picture *Shadow of Doubt*. It was director Alfred Hitchcock's personal favorite among his films.

her twelfth birthday is unbearable to Emily, because, watching from the perspective of eternity, she sees the thoughtlessness of the narrow viewpoint of the living. In the same way, the thoughtlessness of routine existence is unbearable to Young Charlie, because she has a youthful vista of something grander.

Playing Grown-Up. Part of what Charlie wants to transcend is girlhood. She is not yet an adult, but she is no longer a child, and she wants to be seen as grown up. When she parades through the streets of her home town, Santa Rosa, California, with her uncle Charlie on her arm, she does not acknowledge the friends she sees on the street but clearly enjoys being seen with the older man. The situation is repeated in a later scene, when she has a date with the detective who is following her uncle. She clearly enjoys being seen as a woman who can attract men.

Gladys Antrobus in *The Skin of Our Teeth*, though depicted as much younger, shows the same desire to be seen as older and attractive to men. In Gladys's first appearance in act one, her mother scolds her for wearing makeup. In act two she is scolded for wearing provocative red stockings.

Later in the film, Uncle Charlie delivers a speech that is uglier and darker than Young Charlie's, and we see her horror at the same sentiments she had expressed at the start of the film. When she condemns her parents for being oblivious to the miraculous in life, she does not hear the hurtful pride in her speech. She likens her parents to animals; her mother works "like a dog." When she hears her Uncle Charlie express similar thoughts about his victims, denying their humanity by calling them wheezing animals, she realizes the wrongness, indeed the evil, of her earlier sense of superiority.

Sabina in *The Skin of Our Teeth* gives almost exactly the same speech near the end of act two, when she justifies her adultery with George by asserting her and George's superiority over other people. She and George are exceptional people, for whom the rules do not apply. Everyone else is ordinary. In describing the lives of those ordinary people, she strikes the same notes both Charlies do.

These are also the same notes Emily uses in the third act of *Our Town* to describe the ordinary lives of the living: They go through life unaware of anything higher. When Young Charlie makes this observation, she is being prideful and judgmental, but her pride and judgment are merely mistakes of ignorance and youth. Echoed by Uncle Charlie, however, the sentiment reflects the evil pride of the sociopath. Yet again, when Emily laments the lack of human understanding in this life, her observation is made not out of pride, but out of the wisdom that comes after death.

SOURCES FOR FURTHER STUDY

Blank, Martin. *Critical Essays on Thornton Wilder*. New York: G. K. Hall, 1996.

McCasland, Elizabeth Barron. *The Philosophy of Thornton Wilder*. New York: Carlton Press, 1976.

Scott, Winfield Townley. "*Our Town* and the Golden Veil." In *Exiles and Fabrications*. New York: Doubleday, 1961.

Emily, played by actress Martha Scott, is held by her father, played by actor Thomas W. Ross, in the original production of "Our Town" in 1938.

THE BRIDGE OF SAN LUIS REY

Genre: Novel
Subgenre: Historical fantasy
Published: New York, 1927
Time period: 1714
Setting: Peru

Themes and Issues. Like much of Thornton Wilder's subsequent work, this novel explores the relationships between time and eternity and destiny and caprice in human experience. The catastrophe of a bridge collapsing on July 20, 1714, seems to be a random event. Yet to the religious mind in Catholic Peru there are no accidents: All is in God's plan. An observer, Brother Juniper, attempts to reconstruct the lives of the five who perished in the event, in order to reconcile providence with sheer accident.

Each chapter explores a different character's story, but what is discovered in each is not a secret connection that explains random events, but rather eternal truths about human love, which the Abbess calls in the novel's last sentence the bridge between the living and the dead. The line suggests the bridge has a symbolic meaning and introduces a theme that pervades much of Wilder's later works: the relationship between the living and the dead.

The Plot. The novel is divided into five parts. The first describes the tragic collapse of the bridge, the death of the five Peruvians, and Brother Juniper's attempts to connect each death with the moral pattern of the victim's life. Part two tells the story of the Marquesa de Montemayor, who spent her life striving in vain to gain her daughter's love. When finally and suddenly purged of the vanities of that struggle, the Marquesa and her companion die in the collapse of the bridge.

Part three tells of Esteban, whose love for his twin brother, Manuel, is poisoned when they both fall in love with the actress Camila Perichole. They are reconciled when Manuel falls ill, but Manuel's death drives Esteban to bury his grief by going to sea, and, on the way to his ship, he crosses the fatal bridge. Part four charts Uncle Pio's love for the actress Camila. The two have a falling-out, slightly reconciled when she grudgingly allows Uncle Pio to take her son Jaime for

In *The Bridge of San Luis Rey*, disparate worlds and ideologies intersect: Spain and Peru, Catholicism and predestination. Here the Old World and its unyielding authority, resulting in the demise of Brother Juniper, are represented in the sixteenth-century oil painting *Bartholeme de Las Casas*.

schooling. As Pio and Jaime leave Camila, they cross the bridge for the last time.

Part five is an inconclusive summation. Brother Juniper realizes that he cannot quantify providence or even human experience. Yet the book he compiles investigating the stories of the five victims is denounced as heretical by the Roman Catholic court of the Spanish Inquisition. The book and Brother Juniper are burned in the public square.

Analysis. One level of meaning in *The Bridge of San Luis Rey* can be seen in the chapter titles of the first and last parts. Part 1 is called "Perhaps an Accident," suggesting the modernist, materialist view that there is no pattern to the universe. Conversely, the latter is called "Perhaps an Intention," suggesting the religious and rationalist views that the universe moves with a purpose that humankind cannot always comprehend.

Brother Juniper is an ironic figure with a limited point of view, but Wilder does not present him for ridicule. The Franciscan's error is not in thinking that there is a pattern, and the inconclusiveness of his data does not lead him to that conclusion. Rather, his error is the all-too-human one of pride, in thinking that he could calibrate and quantify God's pattern. In the five characters' moments of death, they each realize the folly of pride in their lives, and Brother Juniper follows the same pattern. Thus, the martyrdom of Brother Juniper is not a comment on the tyranny of organized religion, as some have suggested. His death is a necessary part of the plot, for it is in the shadow of death that revelation comes to these characters, and this theme—actually a plot device—is used later in Wilder's drama.

SOURCES FOR FURTHER STUDY

Burbank, Rex J. *Thornton Wilder*. Boston: Twayne Publishers, 1978.

Fischer, Walther. "The Bridge of San Luis Rey and Prosper Mérimée's *La Carosse Du Saint-Sacrement*." *Anglia*, 1936, 234–240.

Kuner, Mildred Christophe. *Thornton Wilder: The Bright and the Dark*. New York: Crowell, 1972.

Simon, Linda. *Thornton Wilder: His World*. New York: Doubleday, 1979.

OUR TOWN

Genre: Play
Subgenre: Modern tragicomedy
Produced: New York, 1938
Time period: May 7, 1901; July 7, 1904; Summer, 1913
Setting: Fictitious New Hampshire town

Themes and Issues. As does *The Bridge of San Luis Rey*, this play deals with relationships between death and life, not only in the final act—in which Emily reappears as a recently dead form of a living character in the previous act—but also in the whole texture of the fictional Grover's Corners, a typical American town in which the past impinges upon the present through the example of ancestors. Relationships among the living are a theme of the play, and they too are affected by death. Mortality brings the characters in *Our Town* to question the drudgery of their everyday lives, the difficulty of communicating love, and the problem of discerning eternal values when living in the temporal world.

Wilder's discussions with Gertrude Stein at the University of Chicago in 1935 and in ensuing correspondence led to his development of a correlation between the individual and humanity in general, which is played out in *Our Town*. Stein's distinction between "human nature" and "human mind" was the matrix Wilder needed to write this play: Human nature finds expression through the individual, but the human mind is universal. Thus, George and Emily are at once individuals and types, Grover's Corners is at once "Our Town" and "Every Town," and the events in the play are at once routine and momentous.

The Plot. Each of the three acts of *Our Town* shows a particular day in Grover's Corners, New Hampshire, particularly in the lives of George Gibbs and Emily Webb. Each scene begins with the random bustle of street life in the town, then focuses on a family scene.

Our Town uses the simple rituals of small-town life to elucidate larger themes of time, social history, and spirituality. As the Stage Manager, who functions as a Greek chorus in the drama, says, "This is the way we were in our growing-up and in our marrying and in our doctoring and in our living and in our dying." Abbott Handerson Thayer's oil painting *A Bride* (ca. 1895; Smithsonian American Art Museum, Washington, D.C.) recalls the event Emily thinks is one of the definitive moments of her life, but when she joins the world of the dead in the final act, her perspective is forced to change.

Act 1 differs from the other two in that it does not describe a milestone in the lives of George and Emily, such as the marriage in act two and the death in act three. Perhaps it is a milestone only in retrospect, for George, not yet fully aware of his love for Emily, is made aware, by his father, of his impending manhood. George, sixteen, is made to contemplate his adult livelihood when his Uncle Luke offers George his farm. George and Emily's mutual interest in each other is evident but undeveloped.

Act two depicts the wedding day of George and Emily as well as a flashback to the moment in June 1902, in which they fell in love. Act three takes place in the cemetery, where the dead sit placidly in chairs, dispassionately observing the living. Emily joins them but is less aloof as the other dead, because she has only recently left the living. She still yearns for the material world she has just left and decides to return to it at a moment of happiness—her twelfth birthday. Her elders in death advise against it, and Emily soon discovers why: the consciousness of eternity makes her aware of the extent to which most of humankind is unaware of the eternal. "They don't understand," is the refrain of the dead.

Analysis. The style of *Our Town* is a deliberate contrast to realist American drama of the 1930s. It is presentational rather than representational in deliberately reminding the audience that they are watching a play and not reality. Reminders come in two forms: first, pantomimed actions instead of realistic actions with sets and props; and second, the use of the Stage Manager as the central character and narrative voice. While other characters are always aware only of their present and sometimes their past, the Stage Manager is aware also of the future. It is this omniscience that links him with the dead, suggesting that the consciousness of death is only one way in which the human mind knows eternity. The speech of the other characters is particular; it is the Stage Manager who speaks of the universal. Through him it is shown that Grover's Corners, provincial as it is, is Every Town.

SOURCES FOR FURTHER STUDY

Burbank, Rex J. *Thornton Wilder*. 2d ed. Boston: Twayne Publishers, 1978.

Cardullo, Bert. "Whose Town Is It Anyway? A Reconsideration of Thornton Wilder's *Our Town*." *CLA Journal* 42 (1998): 71–86.

Lifton, Paul. *"Vast Encyclopedia": The Theatre of Thornton Wilder*. Westport, Conn.: Greenwood Press, 1995.

Scott, Winfield Townley. "*Our Town* and the Golden Veil." In *Exiles and Fabrications*. New York: Doubleday, 1961.

THE SKIN OF OUR TEETH

Genre: Play
Subgenre: Theatrical comedy
Produced/Published: New York, 1942
Time period: All of human history and the present
Setting: Entire world; Excelsior, New Jersey

Themes and Issues. The way in which *The Skin of Our Teeth* deals with the interface of time and eternity is different from the way it is handled in *Our Town*. The characters in this later play are types as well as individuals, but they are also more broadly drawn, almost caricatures. The reason for this is that the style of the play approaches farce, and, as in *Our Town*, characters remind the audience of the play's theatricality. Mr. and Mrs. Antrobus are an archetypal husband and wife. It is revealed at several points that they are in fact Adam and Eve, the first couple. Sabina is the temptress; Henry the mischievous boy, who, his mother lets slip, is actually Cain; and Gladys is daddy's little girl. Time is fluid in the play. In the first act it is geologic, taking in humankind's prehistory. In the second act it is biblical, leading up to the flood. In the final act it is historical.

The Plot. *The Skin of Our Teeth* follows the evolution of the family unit from prehistoric time to the present. In one sense the play progresses through time in a linear fashion, but in another sense all times are equally present in any one scene, and the characters in each time period are essentially the same.

The first act is simultaneously a prehistoric ice age and modern New Jersey. Dinosaurs appear, projections of glaciers are shown, and George Antrobus is presented as the inventor of the wheel. Antrobus desperately tries to save civilization from the approaching glacier and calls on the audience to help.

The setting of act two seems at first to be the commercial beaches at Atlantic City in the early twentieth century, but the scene soon coalesces with the flood narrative from Genesis. Once again George, this time as Noah, attempts to save the world. The third act plunges into the middle of a modern war. Henry Antrobus is at odds with his father, George, and yearns to break free; Gladys and her mother, Maggie, attempt to keep the family together. In the ruins of war, George rejoices at saving his books, with which he will, for the third time, save civilization.

Analysis. Criticism of this play was, for several decades, tainted by a mean-spirited series of articles by Henry M. Robinson and Joseph Campbell essentially accusing Wilder of plagiarizing *The Skin of Our Teeth* from James Joyce's novel *Finnegans Wake*. Subsequent critics have vindicated Wilder, whose borrowings are noth-

Actors Frederic March (Mr. Antrobus), Florence Eldridge (Mrs. Antrobus), and Tallulah Bankhead (Sabina) perform a scene in Wilder's *The Skin of Our Teeth* in 1942.

ing like plagiarism. Wilder openly admired Joyce, on whom he frequently lectured, and connections between the two works may be instructive if taken in the right spirit.

The primary similarity between the two works is their common use of a cyclical view of human history and an archetypal theory of human culture. Certain character types, as well as certain ideas, will appear and reappear at various points in time. The third-dynasty Egyptian, the citizen of ancient Rome, and the modern New Yorker will all be different, but the wife and mother of any era will have certain factors in common with wives and mothers of any other. The play's anachronisms have a comic effect but also demonstrate that character types transcend time to become eternal.

SOURCES FOR FURTHER STUDY

Campbell, Joseph, and Henry M. Robinson. "The Skin of Whose Teeth?" *Saturday Review of Literature* 25 (February 13, 1943): 16–18.

Haberman, Donald. *The Plays of Thornton Wilder*. Middletown, Conn.: Wesleyan University Press, 1967.

McCarthy, Mary. "The Skin of Our Teeth." In *Sights and Spectacles*. New York: Farrar, Straus and Cudahy, 1956.

Rabkin, Gerald. "The Skin of Our Teeth and the Theatre of Thornton Wilder." In *The Forties: Fiction, Poetry, Drama*, edited by Warren French. Deland, Fla.: Everett/Edwards, 1975.

PLAYS

1920　The Trumpet Shall Sound
1928　The Angel That Troubled the Waters and Other Plays (includes 16 plays)
1931　The Happy Journey to Trenton and Camden (one-act)
1931　The Long Christmas Dinner (one-act; as libretto in German, 1961; translation and music by Paul Hindemith)
1931　The Long Christmas Dinner and Other Plays in One Act (includes Queens of France, Pullman Car Hiawatha, Love and How to Cure It, Such Things Only Happen in Books, and The Happy Journey to Trenton and Camden)
1932　Lucrece (adaptation of André Obey's Le Viol de Lucrèce)
1937　A Doll's House (adaptation of Henrik Ibsen's play)
1938　The Merchant of Yonkers (adaptation of Johann Nestroy's Einen Jux will er sich machen)
1938　Our Town
1942　The Skin of Our Teeth
1954　The Matchmaker (revision of The Merchant of Yonkers)
1955　A Life in the Sun (commonly known as The Alcestiad; act four as The Drunken Sisters)
1962　Plays for Bleecker Street (3 one-acts: Someone from Assisi; Infancy, 1961; and Childhood, 1960)

LONG FICTION

1926　The Cabala
1927　The Bridge of San Luis Rey
1930　The Woman of Andros
1934　Heaven's My Destination
1948　The Ides of March
1967　The Eighth Day
1973　Theophilus North

SCREENPLAYS

1940　Our Town (with Frank Craven and Harry Chantlee)
1943　Shadow of a Doubt (with Sally Benson and Alma Revelle)

NONFICTION

1941　The Intent of the Artist
1979　American Characteristics and Other Essays
1985　The Journals of Thornton Wilder, 1939–1961

TRANSLATION

1948　The Victors (of Jean-Paul Sartre's play Mort sans sépulture)

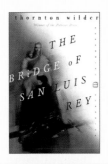

Other Works

THE EIGHTH DAY (1967). This novel more closely summarizes Thornton Wilder's life's work than his last novel. Many of the elements that made his play *Our Town* successful are adapted to the novel form in this book, with some significant differences. Like *Our Town*, this novel is set in a small American town in the opening years of the twentieth century.

Although small-town life is much the same anywhere—and Wilder universalizes in *The Eighth Day* as he did in *Our Town*—Coaltown, Illinois, does not have as long a history from which to draw as does Grover's Corners, New Hampshire, where the gravestones date back to the seventeenth century. Furthermore, Coaltown is dominated by a single industry—the town is even named after it—and the industrial mercantile interests often crush the interests of individuals. Coaltown is a dying town.

A second parallel is the way in which *The Eighth Day* focuses, as did the earlier play, on two families connected, this time not by a marriage but by a murder. The action of *The Eighth*

Claude Monet's painting *Unloading Coal* (ca. 1875; Musée d'Orsay, Paris) evokes the grim, industrialized landscape of *The Eighth Day*, where coal represents the epic sweep of geologic time that predates the characters and will surely outlive them.

Day is precipitated by the killing of Breckinridge Lansing in the summer of 1902. John Ashley is charged with the murder almost immediately, though the narrator states John's innocence, and the rest of the novel is an unraveling of the mystery. This is done through flashbacks that explore the lives of the Lansing and Ashley families, not through years, but through centuries and eons. Wilder covers vast stretches of geological time in a manner similar to the way in which he handled time in *The Skin of Our Teeth*. However, the narrative nature of the novel allows him to interweave much more philosophical speculation on the nature of humankind and destiny.

THE MATCHMAKER (1954).
Several typically Wilderian elements come together in this comedy. First, characters are at once themselves and eternal types: Cornelius and Barnaby, the young would-be suitors; Vandergelder, the merchant; Dolly, the matchmaker of the title. Second, the living connect with the dead. At the end of the play, Dolly talks at length with her dead husband, Ephraim, to secure his permission to marry again. Third, characters acknowledge the audience. Vandergelder tells his life story to the audience in the first act; Malachi the waiter explains his moral dilemma in act three; Dolly hurls an expletive at the audience at the end of act three; and Mrs. Van Huysen briefly turns to the audience in act four to be sure of her own identity.

The comic plot gains complexity and polish through its history of extensive rewriting over more than a century. The play began life as a British farce by John Oxenham, *A Day Well Spent* (1835), was adapted by Viennese playwright Johann Nestroy as *Ein Jux will er sich machen* (1842), and was then freely adapted by Wilder as *The Merchant of Yonkers* (1938), which Wilder then rewrote as *The Matchmaker* (1954). The play remains essentially a farce, with many of the genre's stock elements: the older man who interferes with the younger love interests, mistaken identity, characters hiding under tables and behind screens, a misplaced purse, and a scheming character, the matchmaker Dolly Levi, who plots her own schemes while pretending to help others with theirs.

THE WOMAN OF ANDROS (1930).
As in his first novel and in his play *Our Town*, Wilder explores in this novel the way in which death

Actress Eileen Herlie, who portrays Irene Molloy, appears here in 1955 with Ruth Gordon (right), who plays the title role, in a production of Wilder's comedy *The Matchmaker*.

brings to consciousness the relation between temporal life and eternity. One way in which Wilder conveys this duality of time consciousness somewhat anticipates the anachronisms of *The Skin of Our Teeth*: In describing the moral indignation of the women of Brynos over the exotic temptress from Andros, his language evokes a picture of the modern American housewife fretting over some scandalous hussy.

Another way Wilder unites temporal life with eternity is to connect it directly with death. As she approaches death, Chrysis, the Woman of Andros, realizes at once the pettiness and preciousness of daily existence. It is this rejection of the ordinary in modern consciousness that Wilder later develops in the character of Emily in *Our Town*, and in a very similar character, the adolescent girl Charlie in Wilder's screenplay for Alfred Hitchcock's film *Shadow of a Doubt*.

The plot, taken from Terence's ancient Roman comedy *Andria* (166 B.C.E.), becomes in Wilder's hands a means of showing that a moral consciousness of eternal values is not an invention of Christianity but a part of all human consciousness at all times. Wilder's integration of the theme of eternity is less smooth in this novel than it is in later works: The consciousness that the old pagan order is passing away to Christianity is mentioned in the opening paragraph, and again in the closing, but is otherwise undeveloped.

Resources

The American Literature Collection of the Beinecke Rare Book and Manuscript Library at Yale University houses the largest collection of Thornton Wilder's papers. Included are documents from throughout his stage career, his correspondence with Gertrude Stein, and the original manuscript of *The Bridge of San Luis Rey*. Other sources of interest to students of Thornton Wilder include:

Thornton Wilder Centennial. The Web site created for the centennial celebration in 1997 of Wilder's birth continues to be a useful resource for students and readers of his work. Supported by Columbia University and updated with input from Thornton Wilder's nephew and literary executor, Dr. A. Tappan Wilder, the site contains bibliographies, family information, photos, and comments on all of Wilder's works, as well as links to other Thornton Wilder sites. (http://www.thornton-wilder.com)

Wilder Commemorative Stamp. For the centennial of Wilder's birth in 1997 the U.S. Postal Service issued a first-class commemorative stamp with a full-color portrait of Wilder. It is no longer in circulation but is readily available from collectors. Further information may be obtained from the U.S. Post Office Web site. (http://www.usps.gov)

White House Tape. A tape of President John F. Kennedy's White House presentation "A Night with Thornton Wilder," recorded on April 30, 1963, may be found in the Library of Congress, Washington, D.C. Present were the president and first lady, the entire cabinet, and special invited guests. At the event Wilder read from act 3 of *Our Town*.

JOHN R. HOLMES

Tennessee Williams

BORN: March 26, 1911, Columbus, Mississippi
DIED: February 25, 1983, New York, New York
IDENTIFICATION: Post-World War II American dramatist known for his heavily symbolic plays, many of which were adapted into major films.

Considered among the greatest American playwrights, Tennessee Williams is remembered chiefly for his works from the mid-1940s through the early 1960s. Twice the winner of the Pulitzer Prize for drama, Williams wrote of lonely misfits, sensitive artists, and the sexually and psychically wounded. His most important dramas are the elegiac memory play *The Glass Menagerie*, which debuted in Chicago in 1944 and took Broadway by storm in 1945, and *A Streetcar Named Desire* (1947), about a faded southern woman of grace and beauty who is ravished and destroyed by the brutal forces of modern society. Although his more experimental plays after the early 1960s were neither critical nor popular successes, frequent revivals of his earlier works assure his place among the twentieth century's preeminent playwrights.

Tennessee Williams was born Thomas Lanier Williams on March 26, 1911, in Columbus, Mississippi, the second of three children of Cornelius Coffin Williams and Edwina Dakin Williams. Because of tension early on in his parents' marriage and his father's job as a traveling shoe salesman, Williams spent his early years with his mother and older sister, Rose, living in rectories in Nashville, Tennessee, and later Clarksdale, Mississippi, with his maternal grandfather, the Reverend Walter Dakin, an

Episcopal priest, and his grandmother, affectionately called "Grand." A serious illness left Williams partially paralyzed for two years. During this time, he found solace in a world of books, which he shared with Rose and their black nurse, Ozzie.

The Move North. In 1918 the family relocated to St. Louis, Missouri, where Cornelius got an office job and Williams's brother, Dakin, was born. In junior high school, Williams began writing gothic stories, essays, and movie reviews. His first publication came in 1928, when "The Vengeance of Nitocris" appeared in *Weird Tales*, the same year his grandfather took him along on a European tour. In 1932 his father forced him to withdraw from the University of Missouri. Williams failed to live up to his father's expectations of manliness, and his punishment was working at the International Shoe Company. Later, while recuperating from a heart problem at his grandparents' home in Memphis, Williams wrote a one-act play. He briefly attended Washington University in St. Louis, where the Mummers, an amateur group, staged his play *Candles to the Sun* in 1937.

Apprentice Period. Williams undertook his formal training in playwriting at the University of Iowa, from which he graduated in 1938. The next year, he settled in New Orleans, where he had his first homosexual affair. He changed his name to "Tennessee" when he entered several plays in a Group Theater contest, and the $100 prize he won led to his first meeting with the influential Audrey Wood, who became his literary agent. After receiving a $1,000 grant from the Rockefeller

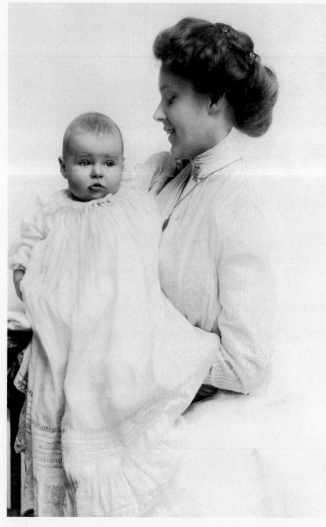

Young Thomas Lanier is cradled in the arms of his mother. His charged, often fraught relationship with his family was to become fodder for some of his greatest dramatic works.

Foundation, he enrolled in John Gassner's playwriting seminar in New York. *Battle of Angels*, his first full-length play, was presented by the Theater Guild of Boston in December 1940, but it had a disastrous run and never opened on Broadway.

During much of the 1940s, Williams was on the road, living in Provincetown, Massachusetts; Mexico; New Mexico; and Key West, Florida, where he owned a home. Late in the decade, he traveled to Paris, Rome, and London with Frank Merlo, who became his longtime companion. While Williams was away from St. Louis, his sister, Rose, underwent a prefrontal lobotomy, which doctors thought would cure her of schizophrenia. Williams would feel guilty for the rest of his life for not having been home to prevent the operation, and he cared for her financially and provided for her in his will.

Triumph at Last. In 1943 while under contract as a scriptwriter at Metro-Goldwyn-Mayer (MGM) Studios in Hollywood, Williams wrote "The Gentleman Caller." Revised as *The Glass Menagerie*, it opened in Chicago in December 1944, where it was kept alive by the newspaper critics; it moved to New York in March 1945, where it starred Laurette Taylor, won several awards, and catapulted Williams to immediate success. His prominence among post-World War II American dramatists was confirmed by a string of commercially and critically important plays and their adaptations to film.

A Streetcar Named Desire, starring Jessica Tandy and Marlon Brando, who became an icon of the youth cult, opened in 1947 and won a Pulitzer Prize, quickly taking its place as one of the most revered American plays. This was followed in rapid succession by such works as *Summer and Smoke* (1947); *The Rose*

A gifted if somewhat erratic and distracted student, Williams poses here for a high school portrait at Soldan High School in St. Louis, Missouri.

Tattoo, which won the Tony Award in 1951; the experimental *Camino Real* (1953); *Cat on a Hot Tin Roof*, which secured Williams a second Pulitzer for drama in 1955; *Suddenly Last Summer* (1958); and *Sweet Bird of Youth* (1959). When *The Night of the Iguana* premiered in New York in 1961, *Time* magazine featured Williams on its cover and proclaimed him perhaps the greatest living dramatist in the world.

Williams also continued to write fiction during this period, including his affecting novella about an aging actress, *The Roman Spring of Mrs. Stone* (1950), which was made into a successful film starring Vivien Leigh, who had also appeared in the screen version of *A Streetcar*

HIGHLIGHTS IN WILLIAMS'S LIFE

1911   Tennessee Williams is born Thomas Lanier Williams on March 26 in Columbus, Mississippi.

1918   Moves with family to St. Louis, Missouri.

1928   Publishes first short story, "The Vengeance of Nitocris."

1936   Enrolls at Washington University in St. Louis; begins publishing poetry.

1938   Graduates from the University of Iowa.

1939   Adopts the name Tennessee Williams.

1940   *Battle of Angels* unsuccessfully produced in Boston.

1943   Williams writes filmscripts for MGM Studios in California; his sister, Rose, undergoes prefrontal lobotomy.

1944   *The Glass Menagerie* premieres in Chicago and opens on Broadway the next year.

1947   *A Streetcar Named Desire* opens; wins Pulitzer Prize and New York Drama Critics Circle and Donaldson Awards.

1948   Williams begins fourteen-year relationship with Frank Merlo.

1951   *The Rose Tattoo* opens and wins Tony Award.

1955   *Cat on a Hot Tin Roof* receives Pulitzer Prize and New York Drama Critics Circle and Donaldson Awards.

1957   Williams enters psychoanalysis after father's death.

1961   *The Night of the Iguana* premieres and receives New York Drama Critics Circle Award.

1969   Williams is baptized as a Roman Catholic in Key West, Florida; enters hospital for psychiatric care.

1972   Makes acting debut in his play *Small Craft Warnings*.

1975   Publishes *Memoirs*.

1979   Is honored by President Jimmy Carter at Kennedy Center.

1980   Tennessee Williams Performing Arts Center in Key West, Florida, opens.

1981   Wins prestigious Commonwealth Award, along with Harold Pinter.

1983   Dies on February 25 in New York City; is buried in St. Louis.

1995   U.S. Postal Service issues Williams commemorative stamp.

Named Desire. He wrote several stories that became sources for later plays, such as "Portrait of a Girl in Glass" and "The Angel in the Alcove" (both 1943), "The Night of the Iguana" (1948), and "Three Players of a Summer Game" (1952).

Personal Agony. By the mid-1950s, however, Williams was suffering from a growing dependence on alcohol and drugs; after his father's death in 1957, he entered psychoanalysis. In the 1960s, his deterioration continued, especially after the death of Frank Merlo, from whom he had become estranged. His brother, Dakin, who had arranged for Williams's half-hearted conversion to Roman Catholicism, had him committed to a St. Louis mental ward in 1969. During this time, which Williams came to regard as his "stoned age," he never stopped writing. His works became more personal in their focus on the artist facing declining creative powers, and increasingly experimental, with characters who were often two sides of the same personality reading lines of dialogue left incomplete. These works were largely rejected, however, by critics and audiences alike.

Even though Williams was long known to be homosexual, the commercial New York theater prevented him from openly handling the subject until *Small Craft Warnings* in 1972. He had forthrightly treated homosexual experiences and characters in many of the poems he wrote over several decades, as well as in such masterful stories as "One Arm" (1945) and "Desire and the Black Masseur" (1946). He would do the same in his longest work of fiction, *Moise and the World of Reason*, which was published in 1975, the same year in which his candid autobiography, *Memoirs*, appeared.

Critical Rejection. Although audiences around the world continued to flock to revivals

Williams donned the persona of the expatriate beach bum in this photograph taken in Acapulco, Mexico, in 1940. "As you have observed," he wrote to a friend in the previous year, "I have only one major theme for all my work, which is the destructive impact of society on the sensitive, nonconformist individual."

of the major works from the late 1940s and 1950s that permanently secured Williams's reputation, new plays from *The Milk Train Doesn't Stop Here Anymore* (1963) and *Kingdom of Earth* (1968; later *The Seven Descents of Myrtle*), through *In the Bar of a Tokyo Hotel* (1969) and *Out Cry* (1973) to the overtly political drama *The Red Devil Battery Sign* (1975) and *Clothes for a Summer Hotel* (1980), all failed miserably with reviewers and closed quickly.

Some time during the night of February 24–25, 1983, Williams choked to death on a cap from a pill bottle in his suite at the Elysee Hotel in New York. Ironically, he was buried in St. Louis, Missouri, a city in which he never felt at home.

The Writer's Work

Although Tennessee Williams wrote long and short fiction, poetry, and screenplays, he is known primarily for his dramas. His major plays from the mid-1940s through the early 1960s established him as indisputably the most important Southern playwright yet to emerge in American literature.

A Southern Dramatist. Williams was transplanted from rural Mississippi to urban St. Louis, Missouri, around age seven. His work constantly reflects the contrast between the two cultures: an agrarian South that looked back nostalgically to a mythical past of refinement and gentility, and a mercantile, forward-looking North that valued pragmatism and practicality over culture and beauty. If the new, northern world exploited the lower classes, it cannot be forgotten that the old, southern one was built upon the oppression of African American slaves.

This tension between old and new is most apparent in the superbly drawn female characters who appear in Williams's plays and are based partly on his mother and sister: Amanda and Laura in *The Glass Menagerie*, Blanche in *A Streetcar Named Desire*, and Alma in *Summer and Smoke*, among others. Economically dependent upon men who idealize them for their purity, they often retreat into a romanticized world of illusion. To compensate for their powerlessness as victims of male domination, they tend to distort by exaggeration normal feminine characteristics, displaying hyperemotionalism, a highly developed fantasy life, and even sexual seductiveness. Often they are destroyed and end by withdrawing into insanity.

Laurette Taylor starred as Amanda Wingfield in the original production of *The Glass Menagerie* in 1945. Amanda can be seen as an extension of her daughter's menagerie, a fragile doll trapped in the world of her own imaginings.

Recurrent Themes. Williams's works, many of which are charged with a highly expressive verbal and visual symbolism, repeatedly explore certain themes and motifs. Williams often makes a somewhat sentimental evaluation of the lost and the lonely, those who are isolated in some way. At the same time, he abhors the underdeveloped heart that refuses to reach out to others who are in need. He sees human sexuality as a means of transcending aloneness, and so castigates a too-judgmental Puritan repression of sexuality.

He is acutely aware of the passage of time, of the loss not only of physical beauty but also of creative prowess and vitality, and he fears the approach of death. However aware he is of intense suffering and final nothingness, he insists on the need for courage to endure, to continue onward. For the writer, this means always continuing to work, since the artistic vocation is viewed as a reflection of divine creation and a means of reaching and helping others in an almost sacramental fashion.

Ever the chameleon, Williams's ability to invent a staggering array of compelling and believable stage roles originated in his own shifting moods and multifaceted personality.

A Poet of the Misfits.

Williams felt himself rendered different, or "Other," by his homosexuality, and thus felt a special sensitivity to all those who were physically, emotionally, or spiritually misbegotten and vulnerable—and therefore somehow special. In an early verse, "Poem for Paul" (1941), which he would later revise and include in his one-act play "The Mutilated" (1966), he asked that succor be shown to all "the strange, the crazed, the queer." Many of his plays focus on those who are marginalized, either cut off from the rest of society racially, ethnically, or sexually, or cut off because of their psychological difficulties or their artistic gifts.

Grace to Overcome Guilt.

If there exists a central failure for Williams's characters, it is their refusal to respond to another person in great need. This undoubtedly reflects Williams's own belief that he had somehow failed his sister, Rose, at the time of her prefrontal lobotomy. Often this refusal results from a character's being too judgmental instead of showing compassion. It is seen in Blanche's disgust over her husband's homosexual liaison in *A Streetcar Named Desire*, or in Brick's rejection of Skipper's plea for help in *Cat on a Hot Tin Roof*. Yet, as Hannah in *The Night of the Iguana* says, in a reflection of Williams's own central ethical tenet, to turn away from whatever is human, no matter how it challenges one's own preconceived values, is to court paralysis and loss of self-respect. Once a character has incurred that guilt, he or she can only be redeemed by the grace of someone else failing them, as they by their lack of responsiveness failed the other.

BIBLIOGRAPHY

Bigsby, C. W. E. *A Critical Introduction to Twentieth-Century American Drama*. Vol. 2. Cambridge, England: Cambridge University Press, 1984.

Boxill, Roger. *Tennessee Williams*. New York: St. Martin's Press, 1987.

Jackson, Esther Merle. *The Broken World of Tennessee Williams*. Madison: University of Wisconsin Press, 1965.

Leverich, Lyle. *Tom: The Unknown Tennessee Williams*. New York: Crown, 1995.

Martin, Robert A., ed. *Critical Essays on Tennessee Williams*. New York: G. K. Hall, 1997.

Roudané, Matthew C., ed. *The Cambridge Companion to Tennessee Williams*. Cambridge, England: Cambridge University Press, 1997.

Spoto, Donald, *The Kindness of Strangers: The Life of Tennessee Williams*. Boston: Little, Brown, 1985.

Stanton, Stephen S., ed. *Tennessee Williams: A Collection of Critical Essays*. Englewood Cliffs, N.J.: Prentice Hall, 1977.

Tharpe, Jack, ed. *Tennessee Williams: A Tribute*. Jackson: University of Mississippi Press, 1977.

Tischler, Nancy M. *Tennessee Williams: Rebellious Puritan*. New York: Citadel, 1961.

Vannatta, Dennis. *Tennessee Williams: A Study of the Short Fiction*. Boston: Twayne Publishers, 1988.

Yacower, Maurice. *Tennessee Williams and Film*. New York: Frederick Ungar, 1977.

SOME INSPIRATIONS BEHIND WILLIAMS'S WORK

Probably the strongest influence upon Tennessee Williams's work was his psychologically fragile sister, Rose, with whom he shared an admittedly strong emotional attachment. Rose serves as the model for several of his female characters who suffer from a madness of one form or another that causes them to withdraw from the world.

Williams also became particularly attached to the works of four writers. He first read Anton Chekhov's plays while he was recovering from a heart ailment in the mid-1930s, and he was particularly drawn to *The Seagull* (1909).

In the late 1930s, Williams visited D. H. Lawrence's widow, Frieda, in Taos, New Mexico. Drawn especially to Lawrence's belief that pagan naturalism can attain a kind of religious transcendence, Williams adapted, along with Donald Windham, one of Lawrence's stories, *You Touched Me*, for the stage in 1943. He also wrote a short play about Lawrence, called *I Rise in Flame, Cried the Phoenix* (1941).

Williams loved the poetry of Hart Crane above that of all other poets. He carried a volume of Crane's poetry with him and used verses from it as epigraphs for several of his plays. He also wrote a short play about Crane and his mother, *Steps Must Be Gentle* (1980), and wished to be buried at sea near the place where Crane committed suicide—though his brother, Dakin, prevented this.

When once asked what he considered the greatest of modern plays, Williams answered, Bertolt Brecht's *Mother Courage* (1941). Although Williams's own plays generally are not as overtly political as Brecht's, some of the distancing techniques that he employs in *The Glass Menagerie*—such as images and legends flashed on a screen—might, indeed, owe a debt to Brecht.

A young Rose stares out from behind the mask of mental illness. The tragedy of Rose, the beloved friend and sister he could not save, is enacted again and again in Williams's domestic dramas, in which unstable women are forced into a hostile world they are ill equipped to navigate.

The Nonfiction of Tennessee Williams

Written over many years, Tennessee Williams's nonfiction not only provides biographical information but also indicates many of the themes and techniques found in his plays.

Memoirs. Like his early drama *The Glass Menagerie*, Tennessee Williams's *Memoirs* (1975) plays freely with time, moving back and forth between present and past. The memoirs also are fueled by disquiet and guilt over his sexuality, which Williams presents in a more "undisguised" manner than he used in the theater. From the perspective of 1972, when he was appearing Off-Broadway as Doc in *Small Craft Warnings* (1972), Williams recalls his growing up and his bohemian lifestyle during his lengthy apprenticeship as a writer. He speaks candidly about his homosexuality, his physical and psychological illnesses, his heavy dependence on drugs and alcohol during his "stoned age" and breakdown in the 1960's, and the critics' lack of "tolerance" for his more experimental plays after *The Night of the Iguana*.

The presence of Williams's much-loved sister, Rose, who was diagnosed with dementia and subsequently was forced to undergo a prefrontal lobotomy, dominates these pages, just as her presence is strongly felt in many of his plays featuring women who suffer from repression and hysteria

Williams's sister, Rose, poses beneath her parasol in this undated photograph. Despite the guilt and emotional blight her illness created, the writer saw to her care and visited her often, her presence a constant source of comfort.

Williams relaxes on the porch in Key West, Florida, in 1956. Despite the public acclaim and the turmoil and upheaval of his personal and social life, Williams still needed silence and isolation from which to craft and create. Key West was one of the settings in which the playwright found repose, a quirky place he always remembered fondly.

and retreat into illusion or madness. Williams's relationship with his sister was the strongest emotional bond of his life, and Rose provided for him the primary example of how to survive "appalling" suffering with grace. Although these *Memoirs* are determinedly not concerned with the dramas that must speak for themselves, many of the same themes and motifs recur here as in the plays: the loneliness and isolation afflicting those who are "different" from others, devotion to the work of writing—which is all he "know[s] of God," the fear of confinement, the importance of honesty and kindness, the diminishment of creativity with the passage of time, and the need to endure in the face of mortality.

Selected Essays. Some of the journalistic pieces collected together in *Where I Live: Selected Essays* (1978) recount events in Williams's life up to the time of his first success or tell of places that he loved (Rome, Italy) or where he lived (Key West, Florida). Most of the essays were, however, originally written as preproduction essays, and they provide insight into characteristics of the dramatic form or of the artist's vocation. Williams emphasizes the centrality

More than just a record of his thoughts and impressions, Williams's nonfiction assumes the dimension of seminal scholarly treatises, valuable documents that provide essential background on some of the greatest American plays ever written. His notes to the original 1944 production of *The Glass Menagerie* offer a rare glimpse into a young playwright's evolving perceptions on theatrical craft. Here actress Julie Hayden, who portrays Laura, is seen dancing with actor Anthony Ross, who plays Jim O'Connor.

of character in his plays. He probes deeply yet understands that there will always remain "mystery" or ambiguity, and that no one holds a monopoly on good or evil. In that probing, artists must be totally truthful and never shirk from showing the darker, perhaps brutal, sides that exist even within themselves.

In one of the most resonant essays, "Tennessee Williams Presents His POV," Williams talks about the absolute necessity to unlock "closets" and reveal what previously has been hidden in human behavior in order for theater to advance. If character is central, one of the main dramaturgical devices through which a play speaks is symbolism. Not only verbal images but also all of those nonverbal elements of drama—objects, gestures, movement, color, light—communicate as directly, or even more directly, as the dialogue. Williams claims not to have the theme that the play conveys in mind as he writes, only the kinds of ethical choices the characters make as they face the corrupting awareness of time and loss. The artist, who is always among those whom society considers expendable outsiders, has a social role or calling: He must be aware of "inequities" and irritate the community by daring to speak out against "prescribed" ideas and by revealing those things that threaten us, be they concentration camps or congressional committees.

Production Notes. Although Williams says that psychologically believable characters are the essence or *what* of drama, it remains for the playwright to discover *how* these characters might be dramatized and made compelling to an audience. To accomplish that, Williams almost always goes beyond using strictly realistic techniques. In his "Production Notes to *The Glass Menagerie*" (1944)—an important manifesto for the modern theater—the playwright expresses his dissatisfaction with any work that depends solely on traditional photographic realism as a means of penetrating to the truth of human experience. Instead, he proposes the need for a transformative, more poetic approach, what the narrator in *The Glass Menagerie* Tom Wingfield calls "tricks" that openly play with theatrical illusions in order to make the audience aware they are in a theater watching a play. Instead of straight realism, which Williams terms "exhausted," he calls for a "new, plastic theater" that is not bound by language. Instead, this new theater calls freely upon visual and auditory elements—image, color, shape, lighting, music, sound, translucent walls—that will help get inside the characters and dramatize their subjectivity.

In another of his essays, Williams names his approach "personal lyricism," a poetic method for letting the characters' inner voices—their "outcry"—be heard more clearly. To a greater or lesser extent, this means attempting in drama something analogous to the first-person point of view and stream-of-consciousness in fiction, reflecting the modern writer's interest in exploring the mind and interiority.

SOURCES FOR FURTHER STUDY

Devlin, Albert J., ed. *Conversations with Tennessee Williams*. Jackson: University of Mississippi Press, 1986.

St. Just, Maria, ed. *Five O'Clock Angel: Letters of Tennessee Williams to Maria St. Just, 1948–1982*. New York: Knopf, 1990.

Windham, Donald, ed. *Tennessee Williams Letters to Donald Windham, 1940–1965*. New York: Penguin, 1980.

Reader's Guide to Major Works

THE GLASS MENAGERIE
Genre: Play
Subgenre: Memory play
Produced: New York, 1945
Time period: 1930s and 1940s
Setting: St. Louis, Missouri

Themes and Issues. The episodic action of *The Glass Menagerie* occurs in two time frames: a present time in which a narrator directly addresses the audience, and scenes between these passages of narration that act out the remembered past in this most famous of all American memory plays. This filtering device suggests a mind trying to come to terms with choices made earlier, and it represents the autobiographical narrator's feelings of guilt over his decision to pursue his own growth as an individual at the expense of the mother and sister he leaves behind.

The narrative passages add a sociopolitical dimension to the play, commenting on the Great Depression of the 1930s, labor unrest in the large midwestern cities of the United States, events in Europe that portend the rise of totalitarian regimes, and the tendency of Americans toward isolationism as they retreat into the world of swing music and romance, blinding themselves to the conflagration to come.

In a dramaturgic device that has proved controversial and is only infrequently used in productions, Williams's text calls for visual images and written legends to be flashed on a screen, perhaps to indicate the way the narrator's mind works by free association and to diminish an excessively sentimental response that would reduce the play to little more than a soap opera about missed opportunity.

FILMS BASED ON WILLIAMS'S STORIES

1950 *The Glass Menagerie*
1951 *A Streetcar Named Desire*
1954 *Senso*
1955 *The Rose Tattoo*
1956 *Baby Doll*
1958 *Cat on a Hot Tin Roof*
1958 *This Property Is Condemned* (TV)
1959 *The Fugitive Kind*
1959 *Suddenly Last Summer*
1961 *The Roman Spring of Mrs. Stone*
1961 *Summer and Smoke*
1962 *Period of Adjustment*
1962 *Sweet Bird of Youth*
1964 *Night of the Iguana*
1966 *Ten Blocks on the Camino Real* (TV)
1966 *The Glass Menagerie* (TV)
1966 *This Property Is Condemned*
1968 *Boom!*
1969 *Last of the Mobile Hot Shots*
1973 *The Glass Menagerie* (TV)
1974 *The Migrants* (TV)
1976 *The Eccentricities of a Nightingale* (TV)
1978 *Bourbon Street Blues*
1984 *Cat on a Hot Tin Roof* (TV)
1984 *A Streetcar Named Desire* (TV)
1985 *Cat on a Hot Tin Roof* (TV)
1987 *The Glass Menagerie*
1989 *The Drift* (TV)
1989 *Sweet Bird of Youth* (TV)
1990 *Orpheus Descending* (TV)
1993 *Suddenly Last Summer* (TV)
1995 *A Streetcar Named Desire* (TV)
1998 *A Streetcar Named Desire* (TV)

PLAYS

1940 Battle of Angels
1941 This Property Is Condemned
1941 I Rise in Flame, Cried the Phoenix
1942 The Lady of Larkspur Lotion
1944 The Glass Menagerie
1945 Twenty-seven Wagons Full of Cotton and Other Plays
1945 You Touched Me (with Donald Windham)
1947 Summer and Smoke
1947 A Streetcar Named Desire
1948 American Blues: Five Short Plays
1948 The Long Stay Cut Short: Or, The Unsatisfactory Supper
1951 The Rose Tattoo
1953 Camino Real
1955 Cat on a Hot Tin Roof
1957 Orpheus Descending (revision of Battle of Angels)
1958 Suddenly Last Summer
1959 The Enemy: Time
1959 Sweet Bird of Youth (based on The Enemy: Time)
1959 Period of Adjustment
1961 The Night of the Iguana
1963 The Milk Train Doesn't Stop Here Anymore
1964 The Eccentricities of a Nightingale (revision of Summer and Smoke)
1966 Slapstick Tragedy: The Mutilated and the Gnädiges Fraulein
1967 The Two-Character Play
1968 The Seven Descents of Myrtle (as Kingdom of Earth)
1969 In the Bar of a Tokyo Hotel
1970 Confessional
1970 Dragon Country (collection)
1971 The Theatre of Tennessee Williams (7 vols.)
1971 Out Cry (revision of The Two-Character Play)
1972 Small Craft Warnings (revision of Confessional)
1975 The Red Devil Battery Sign
1977 Vieux Carré
1979 A Lovely Sunday for Creve Coeur
1980 Clothes for a Summer Hotel
1980 Steps Must Be Gentle
1981 A House Not Meant to Stand

LONG FICTION

1950 The Roman Spring of Mrs. Stone
1975 Moise and the World of Reason

SHORT FICTION

1948 One Arm and Other Stories
1954 Hard Candy: A Book of Stories
1967 The Knightly Quest: A Novella and Four Short Stories
1974 Eight Mortal Ladies Possessed: A Book of Stories
1985 Collected Stories

POETRY

1956 In the Winter of Cities
1977 Androgyne, Mon Amour

SCREENPLAYS

1950 The Glass Menagerie (with Peter Berneis)
1951 A Streetcar Named Desire (with Oscar Saul)
1955 The Rose Tattoo (with Hal Kanter)
1956 Baby Doll
1960 The Fugitive Kind (with Meade Roberts; based on Orpheus Descending)
1960 Suddenly Last Summer (with Gore Vidal)
1984 Stopped Rocking and Other Screenplays

NONFICTION

1975 Memoirs
1978 Where I Live: Selected Essays

TENNESSEE WILLIAMS
FOUR PLAYS
SUMMER AND SMOKE
ORPHEUS DESCENDING
SUDDENLY LAST SUMMER
PERIOD OF ADJUSTMENT

The Plot. Without the narrative segments that punctuate it, the plot of *Glass Menagerie* is deceptively simple. The overbearing if well-intentioned Amanda Wingfield, her dissatisfied son, Tom—whose real interest lies in pursuing a career as a writer—and her painfully shy and slightly disabled daughter, Laura, inhabit a tenement apartment in pre-World War II St. Louis, Missouri.

Amanda embroiders her southern past, remembering rooms full of daffodils and legions

In Mary Cassatt's *Young Girl Sewing in a Garden* (Musée d'Orsay, Paris), the figure is lost in a world of her own, preoccupied by the tiny act of creation occurring at her fingertips. In *The Glass Menagerie*, Amanda succumbs increasingly to her own fabrications. In her hands, the truth can be whatever she determines.

of gentlemen callers before she married a man who eventually left her. She fears that Tom, who reads objectionable novels, escapes to the movies, and surreptitiously writes poetry on shoe-box lids at the warehouse, will follow in his father's footsteps. This would leave her with little means to support a daughter ill-equipped to function in the outside world, away from her collection of old records and glass animals whose fragility mirrors Laura's own. Amanda attempts to relive her life by entreating Tom to invite a Gentleman Caller for Laura. Yet when Jim O'Connor comes, Laura recognizes him as the high school classmate on whom she had a romantic crush.

Although Jim himself has never lived up to his earlier promise, he spouts enough self-help jargon about developing confidence in oneself to raise Laura's hopes; he even dances with her and gives her a kiss. Then he crushes her hopes by revealing that he is already engaged to someone else. After Amanda blames Tom for the debacle, he goes off to join the merchant marine, leaving behind a mother whose dreams for her children seem finally dead and a sister who has been awakened, however briefly, to a physical sexuality she will never again experience. In the narration that closes the play, Tom begs the Laura of his memory to free him from the guilt that has haunted him ever since his desertion from the family.

Analysis. The gently elegiac, or lamenting the past, tone of Williams's much-loved play has tended to distract audiences from its darker undercurrents. Amanda's refusal to face the reality of Laura's physical and emotional fragility and her attempt to retreat to an imagined past far removed from actuality can only circumscribe the present and reduce possibilities for the future. Laura's retreat into a world of imagination, and her envisioning of an ideal to which reality can never measure up, can lead only to her disappointment and disillusionment. A taste of happiness, if it seems likely never to be repeated, is worse than none at all.

Despite his arrival on Friday as a potential savior, heralded by the legend "Annunciation,"

Jim employs his ill-advised tactics as much to charm others as to bolster his own ego, and they wind up destroying rather than saving. Laura's condition when he leaves appears to be one of perpetual loneliness and loss.

The conflict faced by Tom, the play's central focus, between the obligation to develop his own potential and his duty to others, can never easily be resolved; no matter which choice he makes, he will feel guilty. He attempts to work out that guilt through the process of remembering. When, at the play's end, Laura blows out the candles at Tom's urging, it may seem as though the process has been therapeutic and that she is releasing him. The act of extinguishing the candles might also signify Laura's recognition of her now even more diminished and hopeless state.

SOURCES FOR FURTHER STUDY

Bloom, Harold, ed. *Tennessee Williams's "The Glass Menagerie."* New York: Chelsea House, 1988.

Parker, R. B., ed. *Twentieth-Century Interpretations of "The Glass Menagerie."* Englewood Cliffs, N.J.: Prentice-Hall, 1983.

Presley, Delma E. *"The Glass Menagerie": An American Memory.* Boston: Twayne Publishers, 1990.

A STREETCAR NAMED DESIRE

Genre: Play
Subgenre: Tragedy
Produced: New York, 1947
Time period: 1940s
Setting: New Orleans, Louisiana

Themes and Issues. In Blanche DuBois, *A Streetcar Named Desire* contains one of the most indelible characters ever created for the American stage. Williams blends realistic and expressionistic techniques, including lighting and sound effects, to capture Blanche's interior condition. These subtle staging techniques allow the play to achieve a depth and subtlety usually found only in novels.

A Streetcar Named Desire also contains Williams's fullest examination of the myth of the American South, as seen through the eyes of a more materialistic outsider from the in-

The charged dialogue of Tennessee Williams and the fresh and original acting style of Marlon Brando combined to bring a powerful new force to the American theater. As Stanley Kowalski, Brando, seen here in 1951, brought a brute masculinity and a raw sexual presence previously unseen to the Broadway stage.

dustrialized North who challenges the values and way of life of a more agrarian society that is uncritically nostalgic of its romantic past. The play's setting in the raffish French Quarter of New Orleans, Louisiana, allows Williams to bring together on stage an ethnically diverse cast of characters, including—along with the declining southern aristocracy—African Americans, Hispanics, and descendants of European immigrants. The setting also allows Williams to raise issues of economic and sexual power: the way that brutality threatens to destroy beauty, and how cruelty becomes more commonplace than kindness. These are hints that the tragedy presented in *A Streetcar Named Desire* may be the potential tragedy facing modern civilization itself.

The Plot. Blanche, an evacuee from the lost family plantation of Belle Rêve ("beautiful dream") arrives in New Orleans seeking security with her pregnant sister, Stella, who is married to the defiantly macho and crude Stanley Kowalski. Stella and Stanley have a very passionate, if often volatile, relationship, which Stanley sees as threatened by the intrusion of Blanche.

Blanche feels that Stella has come down on the social ladder by marrying Stanley. She sets about trying to create in Stella and Stanley's shabby apartment the sense of "magic" that she needs to sustain herself in a harsh world. Blanche, who surrounds herself with an aura of delicacy and refinement, has also led a life of profligacy and drink. This provides Stanley with a way of challenging her claim on Stella's favor. He questions her possible collusion in the loss of the family home and smashes her possessions.

Blanche suffers from severe guilt over the disgust she expressed when she discovered her young poet husband with another man. Her husband subsequently committed suicide, and—haunted by hearing in her mind the strains of the music that was playing when he died—she entered a series of liaisons, partly to alleviate her sense of having failed her husband. She is unable, however, to find a way of

fusing the needs of body and soul. When she begins dating Mitch, one of Stanley's beer and poker buddies, she believes that she may have found someone who can be "God" to her by restoring her sense of self-esteem through marriage. However, Mitch, very much a "mama's boy," rejects Blanche when Stanley reveals her past sins.

On the night Stella gives birth, Stanley rapes Blanche, claiming that she has been playing the seductress all along. Blanche, as a result, retreats even further from reality into an almost catatonic dream of the past. Stella, taking Stanley's side, consents to have Blanche committed to an asylum. As Blanche leaves the apartment on the arm of the doctor, relying as always on "the kindness of strangers," Stella submits to Stanley's amorous gropings. Though virile, Stanley, too, is vulnerable and insecure; he turns for reassurance either to violence or to a kind of animal sexuality.

Analysis. *A Streetcar Named Desire* displays Williams's mastery of visual stage symbolism, especially in the paper lantern that Blanche uses to filter the harsh light of the naked bulb, which reveals too much reality. Both Mitch and Stanley tear the lantern from the bulb, foreshadowing their psychological and physical violation of Blanche. Williams employs as well a vast pattern of opposites (bright silks versus delicate pastels; jazz music versus cathedral bells) to indicate how fragmentation of experience leads inevitably to destruction. He sets Blanche, the illusionist who believes in the evolution of moral values, against Stanley, the literalist who regards the realms of morality and the heart as expendable.

Whatever vanity and deceit may mar Blanche's character, Williams makes it clear that the Blanches of the world will always be preferable to the Stanleys who threaten their existence. If that were not so, then civilization would backslide into disorder and chaos. Williams believed that in *A Streetcar Named Desire* he expressed "everything" he ever wanted to say concerning the need for mutuality among human beings—for moral categories flexible enough to admit difference and to show compassion rather than judgment, for courage in the face of hostility and rejection, and for accepting one's fallen nature without becoming so mired in guilt as to despair.

SOURCES FOR FURTHER STUDY

Adler, Thomas P. "A Streetcar Named Desire": The Moth and the Lantern. Boston: Twayne Publishers, 1990.

Bloom, Harold, ed. Tennessee Williams's "A Streetcar Named Desire." New York: Chelsea House, 1988.

Kolin, Philip C., ed. Confronting Tennessee Williams's "A Streetcar Named Desire": Essays in Cultural Pluralism. Westport, Conn.: Greenwood Press, 1993.

Miller, Jordan Y., ed. Twentieth-Century Interpretations of "A Streetcar Named Desire." Englewood Cliffs, N.J.: Prentice Hall, 1971.

CAT ON A HOT TIN ROOF

Genre: Play
Subgenre: Social/family problem play
Produced: New York, 1955
Time period: 1950s
Setting: Mississippi Delta

Themes and Issues. Because *Cat on a Hot Tin Roof* focuses upon suspicion of difference—particularly of sexual difference, it might be seen from one perspective as Tennessee Williams's response to the near-paranoia about security during the Cold War and to the congressional investigations that demanded people to name names of those who were "guilty" of certain offenses. Williams's staging puts particular emphasis upon characters eavesdropping and making ill-informed accusations. The play's director, Elia Kazan, urged Williams to write a new third act that would make the ending less ambiguous and more positive, which Kazan felt would prove

more commercially successful with Broadway audiences. Kazan also staged the play so that characters spoke something close to verbal arias, directed out over the footlights, to reveal their interior states.

The Plot. The Pollitt family has gathered at a plantation in the Mississippi Delta to celebrate Big Daddy's sixty-fifth birthday. This turns out to be a death day instead, since word has been received—kept secret from Big Daddy—that he is suffering from terminal cancer. The question becomes which of his two sons will inherit Big Daddy's land. The

The cast Brick wears on his broken leg is just an emblem of the many divisive barriers that run deep in his marriage with Maggie Pollitt. In this still from the 1958 film version of *Cat on a Hot Tin Roof*, Maggie, portrayed by Elizabeth Taylor, reminds her husband, played by Paul Newman, "I'm alive . . . Maggie the Cat is alive!"

older son, Gooper, is a lawyer married to the shrewish and fertile Mae. The younger, and favored son, Brick, is a former football star and sports announcer married to the very determined and tenacious "cat," Maggie. In marrying into the Pollitt family, Maggie left behind a lower economic status. Ever since Brick hung up the phone on his best friend Skipper, who called to confess sexual feelings for him before committing suicide, he has distanced himself and withdrawn from life, turning to drink until his memory is dulled.

In the masterful second act, Brick and Big Daddy confront one another in their mutual hatred for dishonesty until communication is established and certain truths are faced. Big Daddy was himself adopted by the homosexual couple in whose bedroom the action occurs—and whose enduring relationship is described in the most positive of terms. He is not interested in naming the deep friendship between Brick and Skipper "dirty." He is interested, however, in Brick's coming to awareness of the guilt he feels over having failed his friend and of the fear of what that might force Brick to recognize about himself.

Maggie understands that Brick has lost his sense of self-respect and has retreated into passivity. She determines to serve as a catalyst curing him of that condition. To do this, she tells Big Daddy, as her birthday present to him—a lie that is a potential truth—that she is pregnant with Brick's child. After Big Daddy recognizes the "life" in her, she determines to make the lie a truth by throwing out Brick's liquor and locking up the bar. Only in that way can she restore Brick's belief in himself as a decent human being. So it is Brick, in a very real sense, who is pushed to undergo a "birth" day into a potentially renewed life. Big Daddy can now go to his death secure in the knowledge that his land will be passed on to the son who is like himself, rather than to the materialistic Gooper and Mae.

Analysis. Because Williams insists on remaining true to the "mystery" that he sees at the heart of every human personality, he deliber-

ately leaves some ambiguity about Brick's character. This, in turn, has opened him up to criticism for evasiveness and failing to be more explicit about the nature of Brick's sexuality—although the commercial theater of the time almost forced Williams to remain circumspect by keeping things closeted. What Williams insists upon is the need to be nonjudgmental and compassionate to those who are different in some way, which Brick failed to do. One of the recurrent literary motifs during the 1950s was lack of communication. *Cat on a Hot Tin Roof*, especially with its insistence on Maggie's honesty about her own motives, on Big Daddy's right to know the truth so he can face death in the way that he chooses to, and on Brick's recognizing the truth of his complicity, however unintentional, in Skipper's suicide, speaks to the need for openness and acceptance.

The play also raises issues of how masculinity should be defined, and of how the stereotypical need to prove oneself through physical prowess and competitive aggression must be broken down so that other values can enter the equation. The play asks what kind of bonds men can develop among themselves if society mistakes them for something they are not. The play explores power relationships, within both the institution of marriage and larger society, where financial success is built on the oppression of others. Big Daddy, in rejecting the Goopers of this world, seems intent on establishing a more inclusive and beneficent patriarchy.

SOURCES FOR FURTHER STUDY

Clum, John M. "'Something Cloudy, Something Clear': Homophobic Discourse in Tennessee Williams." *South Atlantic Quarterly* 88 (1988): 161–79.

Murphy, Brenda. *Tennessee Williams and Elia Kazan: A Collaboration in the Theatre*. Cambridge: Cambridge University Press, 1992.

Savran, David. "'By Coming Suddenly into a Room That I Thought Was Empty': Mapping the Closet with Tennessee Williams." *Studies in the Literary Imagination* 24, no. 2 (1991): 57–74.

Other Works

SUMMER AND SMOKE (1947). The stage setting for *Summer and Smoke* indicates its nature as a modern morality play. On one side of the park with its stone angel named "Eternity," is the Victorian Gothic Episcopal rectory, suggestive of the spirit or soul. On the other is the doctor's office with its anatomy chart, indicative of the body and flesh. Alma Winemiller, the minister's daughter, begins as a repressed spinster hemmed in by societal constraints. She comes to understand that to be stone, like the angel, is to be bloodless and less than human. Young Dr. John Buchanan, who begins as a libertine, feeding only his bodily needs, comes to believe in an "immaterial something"

that cannot be captured on the anatomy chart.

After Papa Gonzales, father of the fiery Rosa whom John has taken as a lover, kills the elder Dr. Buchanan, the son, now lionized for his medical discoveries, undergoes a transformation and becomes engaged to the innocent Nellie. After losing John, Alma gives herself physically to a traveling salesman. This is not a descent into a life of profligacy but a first step in a journey of initiation into integrated personhood, for if Alma had always possessed spirituality, now she begins to experience humanity more fully. While Williams never denies the existence of some transcendent order beyond the purely physical, the body cannot

Laurence Harvey as Doctor Buchanan weaves a spell of words the prim Alma, portrayed by Geraldine Page, has trouble resisting in the 1961 film version of *Summer and Smoke*. Some reviewers found the inclusion of the "Eternity" angel, a symbol of redemption and mercy, to be overdetermined and heavy handed on the part of the playwright.

be bypassed in order to reach it. Sexuality, too, may be a means of attaining grace.

THE ROSE TATTOO (1951). Williams's most forthright expression of physical sexuality as a means of finding God in another person comes in *The Rose Tattoo*. The play celebrates the victory of generativity over sterility, as symbolized by the onstage dressmaker's mannequins of a bride and a widow. It is also a work that demonstrates the dramatist's "weakness" for symbolism, as everyone and everything seems to be coming up roses. When the voluptuous Serafina delle Rose feels a sharp pain and sees that the rose tattoo has been miraculously transferred from her unfaithful husband Rosario's chest to her breast after their lovemaking, she knows she has conceived a child.

Although Serafina believes the love she shares with Rosario is not subject to time, Rosario is shot and killed while smuggling contraband goods along the Gulf coast, and Serafina miscarries. She withdraws to the house where his ashes are enshrined, closing off her heart until Alvaro Mangiacavallo arrives to help her find renewed fertility. As they make love, the pain in her breast and the transference of the lover's rose tattoo recur. The women of the community pass the rose-colored silk shirt sewn for Rosario but worn only by Alvaro among themselves in a kind of Dionysian ritual. Physical nature and instinct are not only sanctioned but sanctified. Christian faith gives way to classical and even pagan forces that acknowledge the supremacy of the heart over the head.

SWEET BIRD OF YOUTH (1959). One of Williams's most overtly political dramas, *Sweet Bird of Youth* blends two plot lines: the aging screen idol Alexandra Del Lago's attempted comeback and the southern demagogue Boss Finley's campaign for governor. These strands are held together by the no-longer-youthful Chance Wayne, who is Alexandra's current traveling companion and the despoiler of Finley's daughter Heavenly. Williams's long-held conviction of time as the "enemy" of physical beauty, of the compassionate heart, and of the artist coalesces here with an equally strong indictment of racial prejudice.

Alexandra takes refuge from what she thought was a disastrous screen performance

Williams's greatest stage creations are scarred individuals who seek in vain a refuge from their failed visions and unfulfilled hopes. Alexandra Del Lago, portrayed here by Geraldine Page in the original Broadway production of *Sweet Bird of Youth* in 1959, falls into the arms of Chance Wayne, played by Paul Newman. An actress who continues to perform even when the cameras have stopped rolling, Del Lago is unsure anymore how to play the role of herself.

in the arms of Chance, who harbors Hollywood aspirations beyond his talent. A former sex object herself, she now uses Chance for what she can get from him. His response to her desperate need for oxygen, however, rouses her from egoism and temporarily reawakens in her a sense of self-dignity and concern for others. Chance, troubled by guilt over the fact that Heavenly is now sterile as a result of an abortion, chooses to remain and face castration on Easter Sunday at the hands of Finley's henchmen. In the political second act, the morally indignant Heckler manipulates the crowd's reaction at the rally by challenging Finley's portrayal of himself as an Old Testament prophet who protects the racial purity of southern womanhood by embarrassing Heavenly. Like Chance, the Heckler undergoes a kind of castration by being beaten silent and denied a voice.

THE NIGHT OF THE IGUANA
(1961). Tennessee Williams's last Broadway success and the most realistically conceived of his major plays, *The Night of the Iguana* is both a summation of the themes he had pursued up to that time and an indication of a new focus on the artist's need for tenacity and endurance. Set in 1940 on the veranda of a hotel overlooking the Mexican coast, the "cubicle bedrooms" emphasize the walls barring communication between people. The iguana tied beneath the veranda symbolizes beings at the end of their ropes, undergoing dark nights of the soul. The Reverend T. Lawrence Shannon, a defrocked Episcopalian priest who leads tour groups and is accused of seducing a teenager, has always been obsessed with darkness and evil. Unable to see himself as redeemed, he has preached a god of thunder and vengeance.

Hannah Jelkes, the middle-aged spinster artist who refuses to be disgusted by anything except unkindness and cruelty,

acts as a catalyst, helping Shannon to find something in himself worthy of being saved. Only when Shannon frees the iguana, one of God's creatures, is Hannah's aged grandfather, Nonno, able to complete his last and most beautiful poem before he dies. Shannon can now enter into a relationship with Maxine Faulk, the hotel proprietress, that will sustain him and help him reaffirm life. Hannah the artist—both in painting on canvas and in bringing about human mutuality and communion—can only go on alone and endure with grace until she dies.

In *The Night of the Iguana*, the title creature, seen here in Midjau-Midjawu's painting *Birem, Iguana of the Rocks* (Musée des Art d'Afrique et d'Océanie, Paris), becomes a token of the taming of nature. Wilder, more unrestrained impulses are forced to give way to order and reason.

Resources

The major collection of Tennessee Williams manuscripts is housed in the Harry Ransom Humanities Research Center at the University of Texas in Austin. Other materials are in the archives of the C. Waller Barrett Library at the University of Virginia and the Butler Library at Columbia University. Additional sources of information for students of Williams include the following:

The Tennessee Williams Annual Review. This journal, which appeared beginning in 1998 from Middle Tennessee State University in Murfreesboro, prints Williams materials, including papers presented at the Tennessee Williams Scholars' Conference, held in conjunction with the Tennessee Williams/New Orleans Literary Festival each March. Every October, another conference occurs as part of the Mississippi Delta Tennessee Williams Festival in Clarksdale, Mississippi.

Dictionary of Literary Biography/Documentary Series: An Illustrated Chronicle, Volume 4. Edited by Margaret A. Van Antwerp and Sally Johns and published by Gale Research in 1984, this extensively illustrated volume is devoted entirely to Tennessee Williams. Reprinting primary and secondary materials, it serves essentially as a small, self-contained research library.

Video Cassette. A film biography, entitled *Tennessee Williams: Orpheus of the American Stage* and including scenes from film adaptations of Williams's plays, was originally broadcast on the PBS American Masters Series; it is now available through Films for the Humanities.

Web site. The most useful and reliable of the Williams Web sites is the Mississippi Writers Page on Tennessee Williams. (http://www.olemiss.edu/depts/english/ms-writers/dir/williams_tennessee/)

THOMAS P. ADLER

William Carlos Williams

BORN: September 17, 1883, Rutherford, New Jersey
DIED: March 4, 1963, Rutherford, New Jersey
IDENTIFICATION: Modern American poet known for his innovative style and influence on later writers. He was also a novelist, short-story author, editor, critic, and physician.

Merging experiences from his rural medical practice with the innovative ideas of the imagist school of poetry, William Carlos Williams helped shape the structure and content of American verse in the second half of the twentieth century. He influenced later writers on a variety of creative levels, particularly influencing those writers seeking to escape rules established by more formal academic schools. With fellow imagists, such as Ezra Pound and Hilda Doolittle, Williams brought Eastern-influenced forms of poetry into Western literature. By emphasizing themes of American life and using speech patterns of people in his community, he helped open acceptance for writers using ethnic, multicultural, and urban language in the decades after his death.

The Writer's Life

Born on September 17, 1883, in Rutherford, New Jersey, William Carlos Williams was the first of two sons of an English father and Puerto Rican mother of French, Dutch, Spanish, and Jewish ancestry. He grew up in Rutherford within a family steeped in art and literature. When he was fourteen, his family went to live in Europe for two years. He attended schools in Geneva, Switzerland, and Paris, France.

Later, at New York City's Horace Mann High School, Williams showed interest in mathematics and science but also showed an aptitude for language. He wrote his first poem after a heart murmur removed him from sports competition. Around this time, he began rebelling against his parents' rigid idealism and moral perfectionism. His early intellectual indepen-

dence helped shape much of his later prose and verse. Nevertheless, he succumbed to his parents' pressure by going directly from high school to the University of Pennsylvania to study medicine in 1902.

Medical Studies. In medical school Williams had two strong impulses: to succeed as a doctor and to explore poetry. He admired the English poet John Keats and Walt Whitman, the American voice of creative freedom. While at university he met the poet Ezra Pound, who became the most important influence in his life. Pound introduced him to a group of friends, including the poet Hilda Doolittle and the painter Charles Demuth. This little group—unconventional, experimental, and innovative—

This nineteenth-century illustration of Rutherford, New Jersey, shows the part of town known as the Van Winkle block. Rutherford and the surrounding townships would prove to form a lifelong backdrop to Williams's work both as a doctor and as a poet.

became the core of what later was known as the imagist movement. Imagism emphasized breaking away from standard forms to create more vivid, freer styles in poetry. Looking to incorporate the sharp uses of images modeled after the Japanese verse form, haiku, the imagists as a group became the most important poetic revolution in American verse.

Williams graduated from the University of Pennsylvania Medical School in 1906. He continued his studies in Leipzig, Germany, before starting a pediatrics practice at a location near the future site of the modern Meadowlands Sports Complex in East Rutherford. Over the next fifty years, Williams delivered more than two thousand babies and drew from his experiences in all his creative efforts, including verse, short stories, novels, plays, and essays. Believing that a writer should draw from life around him, Williams wrote much about his patients, used local dialects and speech idioms, and demonstrated a marked compassion for his subjects.

By the time Williams entered the University of Pennsylvania in 1902, he was already clear in his dual intention: to nurture both his scientific curiosities and his literary ambitions.

When he began his medical internship in the decrepit Hell's Kitchen area of New York City, Williams noticed the special relationship that doctors have with their patients and found himself hearing poems in birth, death, and human turmoil. As a successful doctor, he was not dependent on poetry for his income and was free to sandwich writing his verse in between visits with patients. He published his first literary work, *Poems*, himself in 1909. His first commercially published book of poems, *The Tempers*, appeared in 1913. He would eventually publish more than twenty volumes of poetry that drew from imagist philosophy.

The Emerging Poet. Williams's relationship with Ezra Pound and the poetic community at large was altered profoundly with the appearance of T. S. Eliot's *The Waste Land* in 1922. On many levels, Eliot's work shaped the global landscape of verse in ways very much opposed to Williams's thought. To Williams, Pound and Eliot returned the emphasis of verse to European concerns with styles and subjects appealing to academics. Williams preferred to use local themes and interests that would reach a more general audience. As a result, he found himself outside the literary world. For twenty years, he received little notice for his work and earned, he claimed, about twelve dollars a year for his verse. He received some attention for his poetry in magazines such as *Poetry* and *The Dial* but spent as much time writing prose as poetry, particularly in the 1930s, to express his views.

Williams's most memorable achievement is probably his five books of poetry about the

Flanked by two actors, Williams reviews the text of his play *A Dream of Love* shortly before its world premiere in New York City on July 19, 1949.

humble and downtrodden northern New Jersey city of Paterson. Beginning with book one in 1946, the epic project was finally completed in 1958. In 1963 the collected books appeared together for the first time. His *Make Light of It: Collected Stories* (1950) included "The Use of Force," perhaps his most famous and most frequently anthologized tale. This story draws clearly from his experiences with young patients, telling how he dealt with a reluctant young girl trying to hide her infected tonsils from her probing doctor.

Rise from Obscurity. Williams worked largely in obscurity until 1949, when he was offered the post as literary consultant for the Library of Congress. That appointment was de-

layed and eventually rescinded because of charges raised against him that he was a communist sympathizer. However, a new generation of poets, which included Robert Lowell, Allen Ginsberg, Charles Olson, Denise Levertov, Robert Creely, and Cid Corman, championed Williams as an alternative to academic systems. Their work echoed his short line structure and sharp imagery, and they regarded him as a personal friend, father figure, and helpful editor. Williams later wrote the introduction to Ginsberg's collection *Howl* (1956), an important benchmark in American verse.

In his later years, Williams suffered a series of strokes and heart attacks. He retired from his medical practice in 1951, turning his practice over to his son, William. In his later works, he

HIGHLIGHTS IN WILLIAMS'S LIFE

1883 William Carlos Williams is born on September 17 in Rutherford, New Jersey.

1897 His family begins two-year stay in Europe.

1902 Williams begins medical studies at the University of Pennsylvania.

1906 Graduates from medical school after making important friendships with Ezra Pound and Hilda Doolittle.

1912 Marries Florence Herman, the Flossie of his later fiction and verse.

1913 Publishes *The Tempers*, his first commercial pressing.

1937 Begins association with New Directions Press.

1949 Williams is offered a post at the Library of Congress, but the honor is rescinded when he is accused of being a communist.

1950 Begins association with Random House.

1950 Receives National Book Award.

1951 Retires from medicine, turning his practice over to his son, William.

1953 Receives Bollingen Prize.

1953 Receives Levinson Prize.

1954 Receives Oscar Blumenthal Award.

1959 Undergoes cancer operation, and his health, eyesight, and ability to speak decline.

1963 Receives Pulitzer Prize for *Pictures from Brueghel*.

1963 Dies on March 4 in the town of his birth.

IMAGINATIONS
William Carlos Williams
Kora in Hell / Spring and All / The Descent of Winter
The Great American Novel / A Novelette & Other Prose

wrote on death, emphasizing the renewing properties of love and the imagination in such efforts as his play *A Dream of Love* (1948) and the poem "Asphodel, That Greeny Flower." Williams earned considerable praise for his later works, including *Journey to Love* (1955), which was deemed easily accessible and beautiful love poetry. His last book, *Pictures from Brueghel and Other Poems* (1962), won a Pulitzer Prize in 1963.

Despite failing health, Williams traveled and gave lectures while working with collaborators on various parts of his autobiography. After an operation for cancer in 1959, he could no longer read and lost his ability to speak. On March 4, 1963, he died in his sleep.

The Writer's Work

Many observers have noted that William Carlos Williams squeezed two lives into one. While his life as a medical doctor inspired his poetry, his verse allowed his medical practice to become art. Williams was keenly interested in capturing the cadences and rhythms of his patients and often scribbled notes on prescription pads between patient calls. He cared for members of a wide range of ethnic groups and listened to and attempted to capture the dialects of black, Italian, Polish, Irish, Swedish, German, and Russian families. Moreover, he wanted to capture a sense of locale in his verse, avoiding images and language that did not reflect the America of his experience. He felt it important for readers to be on the same level as the writer, so he tried to keep his word choices and phrasing simple.

As a poet-physician Williams helped shape the philosophy of the midcentury school of objectivism, which looked for universal ideas from small things. Objectivist writers metaphorically examined patients on tables, seeing verse as an organic entity similar to the human body. Some scholars think that Williams's use of the poor for artistic purposes reflected a doctor's clinical distancing of himself from his patients. Williams's readers, however, clearly perceive his depth of compassion and see his use of artistic forms as logical extensions of his many interests.

Visual Verse. Williams was a central figure in the modernist movement of the early twentieth century. His ideas were influenced by the interdisciplinary interests of writers, musicians, and painters. Williams often said he would have preferred to be a painter instead of a poet, and that his early verse was inspired by his mother's simple still-life paintings.

The visual artists of the modernist school helped shape the interdisciplinary notion that art should be representative of subjects portrayed in words or on canvas, that is, a subject should be symbolic of a larger truth. For ex-

In his role as town doctor, Williams came in contact with a diverse group of people. Peter Rodulfo's 1998 painting *Crowd in a Landscape* reflects the various individuals who helped shape the developing sound of Williams's poetry.

ample, Williams's most famous poem, "The Red Wheelbarrow" (1923), is more than a short description of a simple neglected farm implement. It represents all the labor that depends on it. His use of a common tool as his subject demonstrates the importance of how humans perceive or fail to notice simple things in the world around them.

The visual arts helped shape Williams's thinking from the outset of his career. Most of his poetry from before 1915 is considered immature and undeveloped. His poetry changed after he was involved in the 1913 Armory Show and the New York avant-garde scene, from which he learned about what modern painters were trying to accomplish. Williams was inspired by the innovative works of postimpressionist, cubist, and Dadaist artists of this period. He attempted to convey the tactile and compositional aspects of art in shaping, word choice, and descriptive detail in the poems of 1917's *Al Que Quiere!* and later works. He also became increasingly concerned with typographical matters and placement of words on the page for visual effects.

Musical Ear. Williams was noted for his keen musical ear, and his poetry often emphasized

Tonality, rhythm, a free-flowing form—the world of jazz, depicted here in Otto Dix's 1928 painting *Grosstadt*, or *Big Town* (Galerie der Stadt Stuttgart, Stuttgart, Germany), was a powerful sonic influence on Williams's verse.

sound over content. He was greatly influenced by the jazz of the Roaring Twenties and the honky-tonk pianos that accompanied silent movies. His ear for spoken vernacular and dialect paralleled his interest in home-grown American musical forms. From the 1930s throughout the 1950s, such poems as "A Sort of a Song," "Rumba! Rumba!," "Song (Pluck the Florets)," "Song (Russia! Russia!)," "Ballad of Faith," "Bird Song," and "Song (Beauty Is a Shell)" reflected these interests. His 1945 poem "Ol' Bunk's Band" was a jazz piece written in response to a musical jazz performance that tried to capture something of the jagged tempo of African American jazz.

Williams's interest in painting parallels his claim that he would rather have been born a musician instead of a poet. His musicality is often the subject of critical interest. Because of his use of African American blues and jazz, readers often observe that his form and structure fuse easily. His interest in nonwhite voices and the themes expressed by oppressed ethnic groups merge, for some readers, appropriately with the musical forms of the streets and bars. In fact, this interest began in his childhood when his father read the poetry of the African American poet Paul Lawrence Dunbar to his sons.

Poetic Structure and Innovation.
As a poet, Williams was most greatly influenced by Walt Whitman. He credited Whitman with beginning the search for American verse emphasizing individuality, freedom of expression, and purely American subject matter and voicings. Williams wrote that the most important moment in American verse occurred when Whitman heard the forward thrust of sea waves and incorporated them into his poems. Whitman broke through the poetical structures created by Europeans. Williams himself—more

than any other imagist—carried forth the Whitmanian doctrines, while adding his own individual practices.

Williams taught younger poets to use free expression, encouraged emphasis on syllables in verse, and urged using short-line structures. His championing of Whitman also helped elevate the nineteenth-century poet's reputation during the decades when college curriculums were avoiding Whitman.

Redefining Poetic Forms.
Interested in both subject and the poetic forms used to describe them, Williams was also influenced by the nineteenth-century poet Edgar Allan Poe's

Throughout the twenties and thirties, Williams's reputation was slowly growing, but he always felt himself overshadowed by the candor of T. S. Eliot and other modernist poets. In the forties and the fifties, however, younger writers, such as Allen Ginsberg (above), began hailing his work, citing Williams's rich and simple poetic distillation.

use of the caesura, or pause in the poetic line. While Williams regarded Poe as too formal in his verse, he appreciated Poe's ability to create atmosphere and mood. After deciding early not to use rhyme in his verse, Williams helped move the emphasis in modern verse to line structure and metrical patterns. Like Whitman and Poe, he himself became noted for his writing innovations, notably the variable foot-line structure.

Williams was concerned about the prevalence of free verse in American poetry. He decided that one way to keep the open expression of free verse and retain an order to metered lines was to create the variable foot, by which he meant any poetic measure not fixed to standard beats. Also known as relative measure, the new form was intended to include spoken-word cadences on the printed page. First used in a short three-line stanza form in "The Descent" in book 3 of the *Paterson* epic, the innovation marked that collection as a new step in American poetics.

In order to make poetic lines more appropriate for what Williams saw as a more relativistic world, he claimed the variable foot allowed order and availability in free verse. He said it should replace the fixed foot to represent the American idiom better using a single beat for each line of his triadic (three-line) stanzas to regulate the musical pace of his verse. Some critics immediately denounced the idea, charging that the variable foot in Williams's poem "Some Simple Measures in the American Idiom" was neither consistent nor precise. Others, such as Allen Ginsberg, immediately championed the new form, feeling it opened new avenues to their own creativity.

The Father Figure. All these concerns made Williams a major influence on later generations of poets. In the 1950s, East Coast Beat poets looked to both Whitman and Williams as spokesmen for individuality and American themes and voices. These writers included Williams's Paterson neighbor Allen Ginsberg and the latter's friend, Beat writer Jack Kerouac. Williams's lectures on college campuses led West Coast poets such as Gary Snyder and Philip Whalen to cite Williams as an important influence on their own work.

Later poets wishing to distance themselves from academic formality frequently pointed to Williams as an inspiration. Such poets included the Native American writer Paula Gunn Allen and the feminist poet Anne Waldman. Other poets, such as the gritty vernacular street poet Charles Bukowski, are frequently compared with Williams, who paved the way for both urban and rural poetic expression in freer content and style. Modern readers have come to understand the indebtedness of the American poetry renaissance of the 1990s to the work of William Carlos Williams. His importance was clearly more recognized in the decades after his death than during his prolific lifetime.

BIBLIOGRAPHY

Ahearn, Barry. *William Carlos Williams and Alterity: The Early Poetry*. Cambridge, England: Cambridge University Press, 1994.

Axelrod, Steven Gould, and Helen Deese, eds. *Critical Essays on William Carlos Williams*. New York: G. K. Hall, 1995.

Bán, Zsófia. *Desire and Description: Words and Images of Postmodernism in the Late Poetry of William Carlos Williams*. Amsterdam: Rodopi, 1999.

Conrad, Bryce. *Refiguring America: A Study of William Carlos Williams' "In the American Grain."* Urbana: University of Illinois Press, 1990.

Giorcelli, Cristina, and Maria Anita Stefanelli, eds. *The Rhetoric of Love in the Collected Poems of William Carlos Williams*. Rome: Edizioni Associate, 1993.

Halter, Peter. *The Revolution in the Visual Arts and the Poetry of William Carlos Williams*. New York: Cambridge University Press, 1994.

Koehler, Stanley. *Countries of the Mind: The Poetry of William Carlos Williams*. Lewisburg, Pa.: Bucknell University Press, 1998.

Larson, Kelli A. *Guide to the Poetry of William Carlos Williams*. New York: G. K. Hall, 1995.

Laughlin, James. *Remembering William Carlos Williams*. New York: New Directions Books, 1995.

Markos, Donald W. *Ideas in Things: The Poems of William Carlos Williams*. Rutherford, N.J.: Fairleigh Dickinson University Press, 1994.

SOME INSPIRATIONS BEHIND WILLIAMS'S WORK

No single American poet influenced William Carlos Williams more than Walt Whitman. Whitman's *Leaves of Grass* (1855–1892) dealt with major subjects on an epic scale that set the stage for Williams's own *Paterson* epic. Williams also emulated Whitman's use of the speech patterns and language of everyday people. Moreover, Whitman's interest in American themes and subjects helped move Williams to write about what he actually observed, rather than work with the international scope of his expatriate contemporaries, such as Ezra Pound and T. S. Eliot.

As a leading member of the imagist school of writers, Williams was profoundly influenced by Eastern forms of verse. Like Pound, he was especially interested in the Japanese poetic form haiku, which focuses on simple, concrete images with little explanation of their meaning. Like Pound, Williams believed readers should bring their own thoughts to the written words. However, Williams eventually found himself alienated from his contemporaries because of their championing of Eliot's complex and highly academic style.

Indeed, it might be said that Williams was as much influenced by the imagists for what he did not want to write as much as for what he wanted to accomplish. The success of T. S. Eliot influenced Williams on a deep level, although in a negative way. While Eliot's 1922 *The Waste Land* became the most important poem of the twentieth century, Williams's reactions to it moved his own verse, and subsequently those influenced by him, into a separate tradition.

Walt Whitman was a profound influence on the work of Williams. In many ways, both writers can be seen as distinctly American in their aesthetic sensibilities. In a critical essay, Eric Elliott marks the comparison, suggesting that in his poems, "Whitman presents images of everyday life in America. Like Williams, he possesses an acute sense of the moment. Whitman perceives the external world and distinctly portrays it."

Reader's Guide to Major Works

PATERSON

Genre: Poetry
Subgenre: Epic
Published: 1946–1958
Time period: Sixteenth through twentieth centuries
Setting: Paterson, New Jersey

Themes and Issues. William Carlos Williams's most frequently discussed work is his five-volume *Paterson* epic, along with the unfinished fragments of a sixth volume that were published posthumously as an appendix to the collected volumes in 1963. Williams's lifelong familiarity with the settings, neighborhoods, and lifestyles of Paterson, New Jersey, helped give the series a detail and intimacy that was both complimentary and critical of the town in particular and America in general. Williams's use of the extended epic form allowed him to develop his themes of defining post–World War II American society in ways similar to his historical overview in his 1925 book *In the American Grain*. In that essay collection, Williams described the price America paid for becoming internationally important after World War I.

In *Paterson*, Williams explored the idea that modern progress came at the cost of destroying both nature and humanity. In the latter books especially, he developed the theme of American power producing slums as part of the price for progress. His answer to this social disorder comes later in the epic in artistic, not social, terms.

Another major theme of the poem is that of the poet searching for his own language. This concern with the nature of writing adds a highly personal dimension to a work that might have otherwise seemed general social commentary. On the aesthetic level, the series begins with a poet searching for perfection and beauty but ultimately deciding that humans must settle for imperfection and an understanding of the transitory patterns of life, a movement from idealism to realism.

To make his books topical, Williams said that he inserted scandals of the day to raise reader interest. For many readers, these scandals in the lives of Williams's characters illustrate the problems the poet was addressing on personal levels. The characters and their conflicts make his abstractions regarding art and social concerns understandable and vivid. However, some critics believe that Williams's poetry was too much observation to be truly interactive or personal, and such disagreements among readers demonstrate the epic's wide range of interpretations.

The Passaic Falls in an undated photograph. In *Paterson*, the river emerges as a link between the past and the present, the one constant amid the development and sprawl that arose along its banks.

Williams's 1958 autobiography, I Wanted to Write a Poem, describes how he created his epic poem. He wrote that the idea began in 1922, when the image of a person as a city first came to him. He chose Paterson, New Jersey, as his city because of his familiarity with it and the fact that its history reached back to colonial times. In 1938 he published stories about the same region in Life Along the Passaic River. The Passaic River returned as a pivotal image in the Paterson books. He decided to use the Passaic River and Falls as the driving force and unifying setting in his poem, which follows the river's course through the links between each of the epic's books.

Williams also decided to make his "man as city" intelligent by providing Paterson with a variety of voices spoken by imagined and real characters from the past and present. In addition, he worked a quest in the Paterson epic that paralleled his own life. Thus, Williams used himself as a model for the typical

POETRY

1909 Poems
1913 The Tempers
1917 Al Que Quiere!
1920 Kora in Hell: Improvisations
1921 Sour Grapes
1923 Spring and All
1934 Collected Poems, 1921–1931
1935 An Early Martyr and Other Poems
1936 Adam and Eve and the City
1938 The Complete Collected Poems of William Carlos Williams, 1906–1938
1941 The Broken Span
1944 The Wedge
1946 Paterson (book 1)
1948 Paterson (book 2)
1948 The Clouds
1949 Paterson (book 3)
1949 Selected Poems
1950 Collected Later Poems
1951 Paterson (book 4)
1951 Collected Earlier Poems
1954 The Desert Music and Other Poems
1955 Journey to Love
1958 Paterson (book 5)
1962 Pictures from Brueghel
1985 Selected Poems
1986 The Collected Poems of William Carlos Williams: Volume I, 1909–1939

1988 The Collected Poems of William Carlos Williams: Volume II, 1939–1962

LONG FICTION

1923 The Great American Novel
1928 A Voyage to Pagany
1937 White Mule
1940 In the Money
1952 The Build-up

SHORT FICTION

1932 The Knife of the Times and Other Stories
1938 Life Along the Passaic River
1950 Make Light of It: Collected Stories
1961 The Farmers' Daughters: The Collected Stories of William Carlos Williams
1984 The Doctor Stories

DRAMA

1948 A Dream of Love
1961 Many Loves and Other Plays

NONFICTION

1925 In the American Grain
1932 A Novelette and Other Prose

1951 The Autobiography of William Carlos Williams
1954 Selected Essays of William Carlos Williams
1957 The Selected Letters of William Carlos Williams
1958 I Wanted to Write a Poem
1974 The Embodiment of Knowledge
1978 A Recognizable Image
1984 William Carlos Williams, John Sanford: A Correspondence
1989 William Carlos Williams and James Laughlin: Selected Letters
1996 Pound/Williams: Selected Letters of Ezra Pound and William Carlos Williams, Hugh Witemeyer, ed.

William Carlos Williams
Selected Poems

Edited by Charles Tomlinson

American of his era expanded by the people he either knew or read about in history.

During this extended project, Williams researched Paterson's history, collecting notes that he would later use in several ways. Although *Paterson* is primarily an integrated collection of Williams's verse, it is also a collage of prose passages taken from old newspaper articles, geological surveys, literary texts, and personal letters. Correspondence on which Williams drew range from a letter written by an unnamed semiliterate black man to letters by the poets Edward Dahlberg, Allen Ginsberg, and Ezra Pound.

Letters written by the poet Marcia Nardi provided the voice of the female giant that balanced Williams's giant man. Nonverse material was intended to reinforce the poem's themes and images revolving around the central motif of one man representing a larger group consciousness. For some readers, the voices of other writers and the nonpoetic material added to the complexity of the perspectives and voices of the community. On another level, the extra material provides outside commentary on the verse itself.

The Poems. Book 1, subtitled *Delineaments of the Giant* (1946), mythologizes the elemental character of Paterson, New Jersey. This book is largely set around the Passaic Falls, with the history and origins of the region recounted in old tales that establish the importance of the river in town life. The city itself is described in masculine imagery. The surrounding countryside is described in more nurturing, feminine terms. The two parts are then unified by the river.

Book 2, or *Sunday in the Park* (1948), is more political in its message. It points to the failures of communism and religion in America. Williams also develops his message that an "orchestral dullness" and half-truths spoken by public speakers block creativity and interest in creative efforts. For Williams, redemption from these failures comes from art, imagination, and memory. Using images of a waxworks display, Williams calls his words the

waxworks of his life captured for the reader. Book 2 is the work in which Williams felt that he captured his stride as a creator of poetic form. This book also contains many of his most memorable character sketches, showing his ability to capture the phrasing and diction of different types of people.

The same themes continue in book 3, *The Library* (1949). This book moves from the confused cultural uproar of the mid–twentieth century to the solace of reading books. But the poet sees the past that is captured in published works as resulting only in dissolution and death. The lives of the people described in the early poems are juxtaposed against the desolation in the library. Using images of a warehouse fire Williams had witnessed thirty years earlier, he watches the town and books burn.

Violence is juxtaposed against an African American woman called Beautiful Thing, who cannot speak but inspires the man's passion. This section is one of the most discussed passages from *Paterson*. For some readers, Beautiful Thing shows how the poet used both race and gender in his attempt to portray beauty trapped in a destructive and disillusioning world. After the fire and the rape of Beautiful Thing, the mythical man must then lay his disillusion beside the water of the river when beauty is overshadowed by social violence.

The water motif connects book 3 with book 4, *The Run to the Sea* (1951). This book compares the polluted river with human corruption. Williams finds balance between humankind and the natural world by accepting innovations in science, language, and economics. Expanding the literal and metaphorical horizons of Williams's setting, the river loses its identity when it flows into the sea. The now-swimming man survives and moves inland to begin again. With this scene, the cycle is complete as Mr. Paterson finds his sense of peace. However, the book also ends with an ironic image of an execution alongside the balancing image of rebirth. This imagery shows that the cycle of historical violence is always present.

Williams intended to end his epic with the fourth book but later decided to elaborate on

Williams's poetry is often a testament to the various lives of those he tended as a doctor. Several poems adopt the personas of African American women, like those gathered in John T. Biggers's 1966 painting *Shotgun, Third Ward #1.*

its themes in an unsubtitled book 5 (1958). This volume is usually regarded as separate from *Paterson's* first four books. Its poems comment on the first four books from the perspective of a now-aged poet whose point of view is more international and universal than local. Williams's vision had become focused on the nature of poetry and the beauty of women. He used flowers to illustrate his late-life passion for physical love.

In addition, Williams's view of Paterson had expanded, partially through the influence of younger poets, such as Allen Ginsberg. Through their eyes, Williams observed considerable changes in the social dynamic, especially in African American culture, represented by blues singer Bessie Smith. However, while the poems relate to the setting of his city, the universal character of Mr. Paterson is not present. As a result, the verse does not interconnect as easily as in the earlier books.

A sixth book, unfinished when Williams died, pointed to vigor and vitality even in old age. As the verse of Williams's final decade is

regarded as his finest creative period, the latter *Paterson* poems are more than mere afterthoughts. Rather, they dramatize the aspects of love and beauty without the social criticism of the earlier collections. The poet's voice is no longer one of personal or social struggle but rather one of reflection, happiness, and affection.

Analysis. *Paterson's* first four books describe the city in images drawn from the life of a single mythological human viewing the world around him. For Williams, his mythologized central character is symbolic and representative of the entire city. Calling himself Mr. Paterson or Dr. Paterson, the man-as-city expresses the cycles of his life in ways that express his most intimate convictions. For Williams, Paterson symbolized the typical, self-contained industrial American city, one that yielded both success and misery, failure and recovery.

Throughout *Paterson*, Williams juxtaposes nature with dirty, city images, as when he describes spring bringing both beauty and urban squalor. On the one side are the natural elements and poetic aesthetics. On the other is the community the poet cannot reach with his words. He sees masculine images in urban life and expresses the feminine as nature, especially as flowers. While moving through the seasons, Williams describes polluted rivers and a scarred and patchy countryside. However, he plants the seeds of renewal in book 4 by having a young swimmer walk toward Camden, the home of his mentor, Walt Whitman. For Williams, Whitman represents a poetic vision, a voice transcending ugly human concerns.

The locale is also described in great detail. On one side, Paterson is bordered by the filthy Passaic River, which provides unity and continuity throughout the series. Other natural boundaries include the Paterson Falls, described as the entrance to the city, above which is what Williams calls "the catastrophe" of the urban blight. Across from the bodies of water is Garrett Mountain. By detailing local history, speaking from a variety of perspectives, and word-painting the natural environment, Williams develops the consciousness of his gigantic mythic human.

Critics continue to debate the merits and importance of *Paterson*. Many critics see Williams's strengths as a poet as lying largely within his short, lyrical observations and not in his longer efforts, which often confuse and overwhelm readers. They believe he is most successful when he stays close to local subjects but fails when he tries to make his verse more universal.

It appears that Williams himself was unconcerned with the prose material he chose to insert into the work. None of the corrected proofs of the early books show any marks he made while reviewing the pages for publication. His lack of attention points to his being being interested only in his verse material. In the later books, his failing eyesight may have contributed to his disinterest in closely proofing his work. Whatever the reason, some readers have determined the poetry is worthy of continued study but that much of the supplementary material is of interest only to scholars and university-level teachers.

Some readers are confused by *Paterson*'s mosaic structure, its subject matter, and its alternating passages of poetry and prose. Ironically, its obliqueness and denseness have resulted in

In O. Louis Guglielmi's 1936 painting *View in Chambers Street*, a family makes its way down a shadowy city block. For Williams, the cramped quarters and bleakness of urban life seem a necessary counterpoint to the lightness and beauty of nature. It attests to his skill as a poet that in *Paterson* he is able to celebrate both.

the work's being equated with the complex verse of Pound and Eliot, but in terms far from Williams's own stated intentions. The *Paterson* epic is thus rarely read as a whole in either academic or private settings. Instead, it is more often read in extracts and selected passages.

SOURCES FOR FURTHER STUDY

Conarroe, Joel. *William Carlos Williams' Paterson: Language and Landscape.* Philadelphia: University of Pennsylvania Press, 1970.

Koehler, Stanley. *Countries of the Mind: The Poetry of William Carlos Williams.* Lewisburg, Pa.: Bucknell University Press, 1998.

Larson, Kelli A. *Guide to the Poetry of William Carlos Williams.* New York: G. K. Hall, 1995.

Sankey, Benjamin. *A Companion to William Carlos Williams's "Paterson."* Berkeley: University of California Press, 1971.

Other Works

IN THE AMERICAN GRAIN (1925). William Carlos Williams is known principally as a poet, but his essays on American society and creative forces are also of great interest to students of American thought. The most discussed essay collection is *In the American Grain*. This book tries to define America by examining its history through the lives of such historical figures as the explorers Eric the Red, Christopher Columbus, and Ponce de Léon and presidents such as Thomas Jefferson and Abraham Lincoln. Some of the book's chapters, such as those on Vice President Aaron Burr and the colonial-era minister Cotton Mather, were based on research contributed by Williams's wife and friends. They translated documents not usually available to other writers.

Throughout this important collection, Williams sought to reinterpret contemporary definitions of the American spirit, seeing his country on a personal level. As a whole, the collection attempted to sum up its individual parts into a new American myth. In each essay, Williams was concerned with how American traditions, the form of the essay itself, and modernist ideas of creativity might intersect.

During the period in which Williams wrote these essays—the aftermath of World War I—the United States became a world power. For

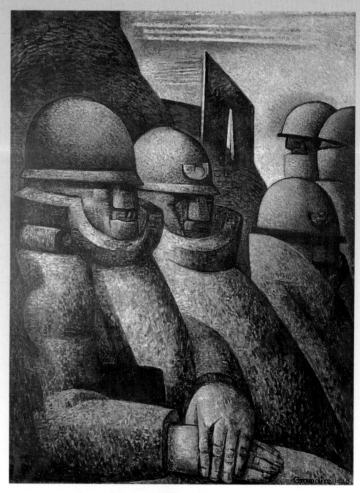

Like *In the American Grain,* Marcel Grummaire's 1925 painting *The War* responds to the dark overtones of World War I. Williams believed the war started America on a path of military dominance it was not prepared to undertake.

many critics, including Williams, the nation's power came at a terrible price. For Williams, the rise of American militarism, the abuses of the Palmer Raids, the passage of Prohibition, and the homogeneity of culture were continuations of the Puritanism of early New England settlers.

In the American Grain also demonstrated Williams's common interests with his friend Ezra Pound. At that time, both still expressed their belief that America needed to change the directions of society and rethink economic policies and practices. Both writers called for breakthroughs in creativity.

SPRING AND ALL (1923).

Few of Williams's verse collections merited significant critical notice as full-length books. Because many of his books were merely pamphlets, that is short books printed in runs of less than five hundred copies each, much of his work only became known decades after it was first published. This was the fate of *Spring and All*. Influenced by French writers and Dadaist painters, this fusion of prose and verse was noted for the Eastern-influenced theme of investigating the oneness of life. Its verses stressed the individuality of human life in individual moments, pointing to how particular subjects could be expanded into universal concepts through the imagination.

In *Spring and All*, Williams let the human condition speak for itself by using the voices of different characters, rather than commenting on humankind from an omniscient point of view.

The last of his experimental verse collections, it reflected the influence of T. S. Eliot by challenging Eliot's more pessimistic view of the age. Williams instead pointed to the self-reliant, compassionate vision inspired by Walt Whitman. He rejected Eliot's theme of alienation in favor of affirmation of the imagination breaking through barriers. His social concerns were also evident when he observed "the chill of reality" could chill the individual poem.

WHITE MULE (1937).

Although Williams's attempts at fiction were less successful than his poetry, his novels are still read as keys to un-

In his fiction, Williams counterbalances an idealized American childhood with the sweeping social changes that were to come in the twentieth century. Edvard Munch's *Two Girls with Blue Aprons* (Munch Museet, Oslo) suggests the youthful innocence of Flossie and Lottie in *White Mule*.

derstanding the themes in his verse. He wrote a trilogy of novels while his poetic output was dwindling: *White Mule, In the Money* (1940), and *The Build-up* (1952). He based these books on his wife Flossie's family. In these explorations of change in the American social climate, Williams compared the childhoods of Flossie and Lottie Stecher with the youthful hopefulness of new American immigrants.

White Mule, the first volume of the trilogy, is generally considered the best of the three. It synthesized Flossie's childhood and Williams's own experiences as a pediatrician, using an ob-jective third-person narrator. This use of personal experience resulted in a detailed and believable account of youth. This book's sequel, *In the Money*, is also set during Flossie's early years but moves into more general themes. In it, the drive for success and competition in the twentieth-century American home is juxtaposed against the nonmaterial drive to do good workmanship. The final novel, *The Build-Up*, moves William's characters into the suburbs, where Williams reflects a fondness for middle-class values while critiquing the pettiness of complacent lifestyles.

Resources

Kent University's Department of Special Collections and Archives contains a collection of William Carlos Williams's manuscripts, a critical essay, and correspondence. Information may be found on line (http://www.library.kent.edu/speccoll/literature/poetry/williams.html). Other sources of interest include

William Carlos Williams Review. The University of Texas at Austin publishes a biannual publication on Williams. The site features samples from current and back issues along with subscription information. (http://www.en.utexas.edu/wcw/index2.html)

Annenberg/CPB Multimedia Collection. A rendition of the poem "The Great Figure" is available in the *Voices & Visions* video series. The one-hour *Voices & Visions* video biography is widely available in public and school libraries, and it is an excellent resource. (http://www.learner.org/collections/multimedia/literature/vvseries/vvspot/Williams.html)

The Academy of American Poets, Poetry Exhibits, William Carlos Williams. This Web site includes a brief biography and a selected bibliography of Williams's works and on-line exhibits at the American Academy of American Poets site. This site is linked to important Web pages associated with Williams. (http://www.poets.org/LIT/POET/Wcwilfst.htm)

Gale Poetry Resource Center: William Carlos Williams. This site provides a detailed biography and an assortment of analytical and critical studies of Williams's work. (http://www.gale.com/library/resrcs/poets_cn/wilmsbio.htm)

Modern American Poetry. William Carlos Williams. Compiled by Cary Nelson, this Web site contains a collection of critical, historical, and biographical information. (http://www.english.uiuc.edu/maps/poets/s_z/williams/williams.htm)

WESLEY BRITTON

Richard Wright

BORN: September 4, 1908, near Natchez, Mississippi
DIED: November 28, 1960, Paris, France
IDENTIFICATION: Mid-twentieth-century African American writer noted for his social realism.

Richard Wright was the first twentieth-century African American writer to gain national literary prominence, and he served as a mentor to African American writers who followed him, such as James Baldwin and Ralph Ellison. Wright wrote both short and long fiction as well as essays and auto-biography. His early stories, collected in *Uncle Tom's Children* (1938), won many awards, and his subsequent novel, *Native Son*, was a best-seller in 1940. In 1945 Wright published *Black Boy*, which has been studied for decades as a model of autobiography. Wright realistically depicted the struggle of African Americans in the early twentieth-century United States to confront and over-come oppression and violence.

The Writer's Life

Richard Wright was born in 1908 on a farm outside Natchez, Mississippi, where his father, Nathan, was a sharecropper. Forced off his land when the price of cotton dropped in 1912, Wright's father moved his family to Memphis, Tennessee but soon deserted them, leaving his wife, Ella, Richard, and Richard's younger brother, Alan, to fend for themselves. While living with his maternal grandmother, Wright accidentally set fire to her house, a memory that would haunt him throughout his

life. For the next few years, Wright and his mother and brother were dependent on various relatives for survival.

Childhood. Wright's early years were not happy ones, as he makes clear in his autobiography. His father abandoned the family, and his mother was sick much of the time. Although he attended school irregularly when he was younger, he graduated as valedictorian from the Smith-Robinson Public School in Jackson, Mississippi, in 1925. Alienated from his extended family by their religious fundamentalism and from any further education by his poverty, Wright began working at a series of odd jobs, earning enough money to move back to Memphis. He also began to read with a purpose. As he related in *Black Boy*, Wright forged a note to the librarian at the all-white city library that allowed him to discover the realist writers such as Stephen Crane, Theodore Dreiser, and Sinclair Lewis, who would help to shape his fiction.

Chicago and Communism. In December of 1927 Wright moved to Chicago, where his mother and brother were soon able to join him. He again held a series of short-term jobs—postal clerk, insurance agent—during the Great Depression. He continued to write, and finally found work with the Illinois Federal Writers' Project, one of many programs established to aid artists during the 1930s under the federal government's Works Progress Administration

The frailty and poor health of Wright's mother, Ella, often created tension and distance between the two. In *Black Boy* he writes, "All morning my mother had been scolding me, telling me to keep still, warning me that I must make no noise. And I was angry, fretful, and impatient."

(WPA). He also began attending meetings of the John Reed Club, a literary organization sponsored by the Communist Party. Through the John Reed Club, Wright began publishing stories and poems in a number of left-wing magazines, including *Left Front*. His powerful poem "I Have Seen Black Hands," appeared in *New Masses* in June of 1934. He also joined the Communist Party, which, in the first half of the 1930s, was working actively on racial problems in the United States. Wright became the executive secretary of the John Reed Club and continued to publish fiction, poetry, and essays.

Chicago, as seen looking south along Michigan Boulevard in 1927, the year Richard Wright moved there with his family. It was there that he first began to think of himself as a full-fledged writer.

New York and Success.

In May of 1937 Richard Wright moved to New York to assume the position of Harlem editor for the *Daily Worker*, the major communist newspaper in the United States. His short-story collection *Uncle Tom's Children* was published the following year and won a $500 *Story* magazine prize for the best work from the Federal Writers' Project. Wright had become a well-known American writer, and with a Guggenheim Fellowship that allowed him the freedom to finish his novel *Native Son*, Wright married Rose Dhima Meadman in 1939.

In 1940 *Native Son* was published, to popular and critical acclaim. Wright was having less success in his personal life, however. He and his wife moved to Cuernavaca, Mexico, for a few months, but Wright soon returned alone; later that year he and his wife were divorced. On March 12, 1941, Wright married Ellen Poplar, and the next year their daughter Julia was born. He continued to write and publish, collaborating on *Twelve Million Black Voices* (1941), a pictorial history of African Americans, and cowriting with Paul Green the dramatic version of *Native Son: The Biography of a Young American* (1941), produced on Broadway by Orson Welles's Mercury Theatre.

Early in 1945 Wright published *Black Boy*, the first half of his autobiography—a story that took him through his first nineteen years of life, before his move to Chicago and literary fame. Like *Native Son*, the work was selected by the Book-of-the-Month Club and won immediate acclaim. Wright bought a home in New York City's Greenwich Village. A few months later he accepted an invitation to visit France for three months, sailing there in May of 1946. Recognizing the vast differences in the two countries' treatment of blacks, Wright returned to New York to sell his home. He resettled in France in 1947 and soon became a member of Parisian literary circles, befriending important French writers, including Jean-Paul Sartre and Simone de Beauvoir.

The now successful writer poses with his second wife, Ellen, in this photograph from the 1940s.

Exile. Wright would live out his remaining years abroad, his most important literary productions behind him. His second daughter, Rachel, was born in France in 1949, while Wright was working on a film version of *Native Son* (1950) with himself in the lead role. In 1953, he published *The Outsider*, a novel that had clearly been influenced by his experiences in the existentialist literary circles in Paris. Increasingly, Wright was drawn to Africa, and he spent three months there in 1953. He would publish a series of volumes in his last years, most of them based on his travels—to Africa, Spain, Indonesia—but novels, too. Wright bought a farm in Normandy in 1955 but in 1959 sold it and moved to London, England. When he failed to gain a permanent visa in England, he returned to Paris, where he died of heart failure on November 28, 1960.

This 1943 photograph captures Wright in a pensive moment in his study. As his success grew, it became all the more crucial to the author to have a quiet haven in which to write and think.

HIGHLIGHTS IN WRIGHT'S LIFE

1908 Richard Wright is born on September 4 on a farm near Natchez, Mississippi.

1912 Family moves to maternal grandmother's home, which Wright accidentally sets on fire.

1914 Father deserts family when Wright is six.

1916–1925 Wright attends school sporadically, graduating as valedictorian.

1926 Holds a series of odd jobs and reads intensely.

1927 Moves to Chicago, where he becomes an active writer and holds a number of jobs.

1932 Attends meetings of the John Reed Club; begins publishing in left-wing magazines.

1934 Joins the Communist Party.

1937 Becomes Harlem editor of the *Daily Worker*.

1938 Publishes *Uncle Tom's Children* to wide praise.

1939 Receives Guggenheim Fellowship; marries Rose Dhima Meadman.

1940 Publishes best-seller *Native Son*; is divorced from Meadman.

1941 Marries Ellen Poplar.

1942 Daughter Julia is born; Wright resigns from the Communist Party.

1945 Wright publishes *Black Boy*.

1947 Leaves United States to settle in France.

1949 Daughter Rachel is born; Wright works on film version of *Native Son*.

1953 Publishes *The Outsider*; visits Africa.

1954 Publishes *Black Power: A Record of Reactions in a Land of Pathos* and *Savage Holiday*; visits Spain.

1955 Attends the Bandung Conference in Indonesia.

1956 Publishes *The Color Curtain: A Report on the Bandung Conference*.

1957 Publishes *Pagan Spain* and *White Man, Listen!*.

1958 Publishes novel *The Long Dream*.

1960 Dies of heart failure in Paris, France, on November 28.

1961 *Eight Men* is published posthumously.

The Writer's Work

While Richard Wright published numerous literary works, he is best known for single works in three different genres: a collection of short stories, *Uncle Tom's Children*; a novel, *Native Son*; and an autobiography, *Black Boy*. In these three works, published within a span of eight years, Wright delineated a number of important issues facing the United States in the mid–twentieth century and influenced future discussion of those issues. The critic Arnold Rampersad noted that Wright's work is significant because it cast an extraordinary light on the place of African Americans in the national consciousness.

Issues in Wright's Fiction. The major but by no means only issues in Wright's books are racial. While Wright's fiction and his autobiography graphically describe the conditions in which African Americans lived in the first half of the twentieth century and their uneasy relations with whites, other overriding issues emerge. Wright is clearly a naturalistic writer, and his fiction recalls the work of Theodore Dreiser, Sinclair Lewis, and others, as well as that of his close contempory John Steinbeck. These writers are known for their treatment of the forces that tend to control the lives of their characters—environmental (as in Steinbeck's *The Grapes of Wrath*, 1939), economic (as in Upton Sinclair's *The Jungle*, 1906), or psychological (as in Stephen Crane's *Red Badge of Courage*, 1895).

When critics use the term *existential* to describe Richard Wright, however, they are pointing to the ways in which Wright's work applies to *all* people and not just one racial group. The dilemmas of his characters—trapped within worlds they did not create—symbolize the condition of the broadest spectrum of Americans of all colors and classes. What stands out in Wright's fiction, in short, is the way in which his black characters' situations raise issues of universal relevance.

People in Wright's Fiction. Wright's characters are often but not always black and poor, for example, Big Boy in "Big Boy Leaves Home," Bigger Thomas in *Native Son*, and Dave in "The Man Who Was Almost a Man." While these characters elicit sympathy because of their entrapment in either the

Here Wright works at home on one of his favorite old typewriters.

country or the city, at the same time they often repel readers by the ways in which they answer violence with violence. Likewise, Wright has been faulted for the limitations of his female characters, who tend to be two-dimensional victims. Still, such characterization is the weakness of the naturalist mode, in which characters often represent social and psychological forces as much as real human figures. Wright's own feeling for black characters can be seen most clearly in *Twelve Million Black Voices*, a pictorial history of African Americans in which, with photographs from the Farm Security Administration, Wright's third-person plural voice links him with disenfranchised blacks throughout American history.

Wright's Imagery. Wright's prose is powerful not only because of the violence and brutality it depicts but also because of the brilliant way that metaphors and motifs convey his meaning. Fire and water, for instance, figure strongly in such stories as "Down by the Riverside" and "Fire and Cloud" from *Uncle Tom's Children*, where they carry an almost biblical significance. The image of underground characters—such as Big Boy or Fred Daniels in "The Man Who Lived Underground"—represent the entrapment of these characters in physical environments and raise the larger existential question of how they can free themselves from such prisons. Wright's prose is often raw in emotion and colloquial in dialogue, but his manipulation of language and image reveals a deliberate and remarkable ability.

In Julia Condon's 1997 painting *Flame Emerging from Water,* fire dances delicately on the surface of a pool. These two elements permeate Wright's stories, from which the flame emerges as an image of power and endurance, a spirit that cannot be extinguished.

Literary Legacy. It is noteworthy that the two most important African American writers to follow Wright—Ralph Ellison and James Baldwin—felt compelled to note his limitations and define themselves against his achievements, almost like sons trying to establish their identities in the shadow of a strong father. Ellison's and Baldwin's attacks demonstrate the continuing power of Wright's prose. Other writers who followed for the next fifty years in the genres Wright mastered were forced, if not to acknowledge his literary influence, then at least to confront his remarkable legacy.

SOME INSPIRATIONS BEHIND WRIGHT'S WORK

As Richard Wright influenced generations of writers who followed him, he too was shaped by a number of important American writers, from at least four separate periods. His debt to the literary naturalists, such as Stephen Crane and Frank Norris, is obvious. Wright himself wrote, however, that he hoped to be ranked with earlier, nineteenth-century writers such as Edgar Allan Poe and Nathaniel Hawthorne, and his prose certainly has some of their romantic elements.

While Wright's fiction is clearly indebted to the postwar French existentialists Jean-Paul Sartre and Albert Camus, he was also familiar with the earlier twentieth-century Anglo-American modernists, such as Gertrude Stein, James Joyce, William Faulkner, and Ernest Hemingway. Wright's first novel, *Lawd Today*, written in the mid-1930s but not published until after his death in 1963, reveals the influences of Joyce and other modernist writers. Even *White Man, Listen!*, one of the most political of Wright's books, begins with epigraphs from the poets William Blake and Dylan Thomas.

Several of these influences are described in the famous passage in *Black Boy* when Wright forges a note to a white librarian in order to borrow books. The iconoclastic literary critic H. L. Mencken led Wright to other early twentieth-century realist writers, such as Sinclair Lewis and Theodore Dreiser, and also to Joseph Conrad, Gustave Flaubert, Bernard Shaw, and T. S. Eliot.

The ruminating, almost existentialist tone that colors some of Wright's work echoes the writing of Jean-Paul Sartre, shown here (center) lunching in Paris in 1964 with writer Simone de Beauvoir (right).

BIBLIOGRAPHY

Bloom, Harold, ed. *Richard Wright*. New York: Chelsea House, 1987.

Butler, Robert. *The Critical Response to Richard Wright*. Westport, Conn.: Greenwood Press, 1995.

Campbell, James. *Exiled in Paris: Richard Wright, James Baldwin, Samuel Beckett, and Others on the Left Bank*. New York: Scribner's, 1995.

Fabre, Michel. *The Unfinished Quest of Richard Wright*. New York: Morrow, 1973.

Felgar, Robert. *Richard Wright*. Boston: Twayne Publishers, 1980.

Gates, Henry Louis, Jr., and K. A. Appiah, eds. *Richard Wright: Critical Perspectives Past and Present*. New York: Penguin, 1993.

Hakutani, Yoshinobu. *Richard Wright and Racial Discourse*. St. Louis: University of Missouri Press, 1996.

Joyce, Joyce Ann. *Richard Wright's Art of Tragedy*. Iowa City: University of Iowa Press, 1986.

Kinnamon, Keneth, and Michel Fabre, eds. *Conversations with Richard Wright*. Jackson: University of Mississippi Press, 1993.

Macksey, Richard, and Frank E. Moorer, eds. *Richard Wright: A Collection of Critical Essays*. Englewood Cliffs, N.J.: Prentice-Hall, 1984.

Rampersad, Arnold, ed. *Richard Wright: A Collection of Critical Essays*. Englewood Cliffs, N.J.: Prentice Hall, 1995.

Walker, Margaret. *Richard Wright: Daemonic Genius*. New York: Warner Books, 1988

Reader's Guide to Major Works

BLACK BOY

> **Genre:** Nonfiction
> **Subgenre:** Autobiography
> **Published:** New York, 1945
> **Time period:** 1912 to 1927
> **Setting:** Southern United States; Chicago, Illinois

Themes and Issues. When Richard Wright submitted the manuscript of his autobiography, the publishers asked him to drop the second half, and he complied. Pieces of the second half appeared during his lifetime, but the entire second part was not published until 1977, when it was released as *American Hunger*. In most subsequent editions of *Black Boy* (and especially after the Library of America edition of Wright's works in 1991), the second half has been restored, and the complete work is titled *Black Boy (American Hunger)* and subtitled *A Record of Childhood and Youth*.

Black Boy's two books are named "Southern Nights" and "The Horror and the Glory," respectively, and break on his departure for Chicago. In spite of this convoluted publishing history, *Black Boy*, in its various mutations, has

In a 1945 interview Wright said, "I know that the scalding experiences of *Black Boy* are alien to most Americans to whom education is a matter-of-course thing, to whom food is something to be taken for granted, to whom freedom is a heritage." He wrote his autobiography partially as an attempt to expose the poverty, racism, and lack of opportunity that punctuated the lives of many black children in the South.

become one of the landmarks of American auto-biography, and it is read and studied with other classics of the genre, such as *The Autobiography of Benjamin Franklin* (1771–1789), Frederick Douglass's *Narrative of the Life of Frederick Douglass, an American Slave, Written by Himself* (1845), and Mark Twain's *Old Times on the Mississippi* (1875).

Wright's *Black Boy* raises many of the same issues that his fiction does: the plight of African Americans in the South, their flight to the North, and the violence and brutality that invade their lives. *Black Boy* can be seen as the nonfictional underpinning of Wright's novels and short stories, with the qualification that the line between Wright's fiction and nonfiction is very thin. His fiction draws heavily on his own experience, and his autobiography is full of exaggerations and fabrications. In consequence, the two literary forms can be discussed using almost the same critical terms. New themes that are foremost in *Black Boy* include that of the American Dream, the struggle for self-creation, the personal tension between freedom and control, and the power of language.

The Plot. The book is almost relentlessly shocking, beginning in the first scene, when the four-year-old Wright sets fire to his grandmother's house. The early chapters of *Black Boy* depict vividly both Wright's specific personal plight (hunger, his mother's illness, his father's desertion) and the general struggles of southern blacks (particularly the killing of Uncle Hoskins by the "white terror"). If "Southern Nights" has a plot, it is one of Wright's self-discovery, his family's unre-

liability and religious fundamentalism, and his sporadic attempts at education. At the same time, he describes the white world in which he holds a series of odd jobs and the violence that may erupt there at any time. The young Richard Wright is developing between the poles of two irrational and violent worlds.

After Wright's graduation from high school, his focus shifts more and more to the white world in which he works and the dangers that lurk there. In just one of many notable incidents, Wright is accused of looking at a naked white prostitute in the hotel where he is a bell-hop and realizes the necessity of learning how to navigate this threatening world. Toward the

In William H. Johnson's *Chain Gang* (National Museum of American Art, Washington, D.C.), prisoners toil in the hot sun. The theme of entrapment—spiritual and physical—is central to *Black Boy.* The art of writing, the ability to articulate one's alienation and imprisonment, becomes in the work a powerful act of freedom.

end of book 1, Wright flees to Memphis, Tennessee, where he still feels hungry and trapped but is able to forge a note to the white librarian to gain access to great books and begin his real self-education. Book 1 closes with a meditation on the difficulties of his position and his limited options in this world.

Book 2, "The Horror and the Glory," opens with "My first glimpse of the flat black stretches of Chicago. . . ." Wright has escaped the South but not the dilemma of being a black American. What he discovers in Chicago is that his alienation is not geographical but racial: "I had fled one insecurity and had embraced another." There are more such sociological and psychological analyses in the second book of *Black Boy*, as an older Richard Wright tries to understand his difficult situation. He is able to get a series of temporary jobs—clerking at the post office, selling insurance—but during the worst of the Great Depression, in 1932, he is on relief.

His personal relief comes when he discovers the John Reed Club, a literary organization sponsored by the Communist Party, and publishes his first stories. However, Wright soon grows disillusioned with the Communist Party that had first supported him. He finds work in the Federal Writers' Project, but when he tries to march in the May Day parade, he is physically thrown out by party members. Wright has begun his life as a writer, and the book ends with his promise, "I would hurl words into this darkness and wait for an echo, and if an echo sounded, no matter how faintly, I would send other words to tell, to march, to fight, to create a sense of the hunger for life that gnaws in us all, to keep alive in our hearts a sense of the inexpressibly human."

Analysis. The incidents of this life story are told in a vivid prose that most commentators praise for its lyrical sounds reminiscent of blues music. *Black Boy* is a work of power that raises some of the most important racial issues of American life. Many of those issues, as previously noted, are those that readers also find in Wright's fiction, particularly the African American struggle for survival and dignity against oppression. In *Black Boy*, Wright adds analysis explaining his understanding of these conditions. While some critics balk at the text's sociology, it is essential to the reader's understanding of the racial oppression, social determinism, and self-creation in Wright's life story. In many ways Wright's story parallels the plot of the nineteenth-century slave narrative.

Because this is a work of art and not a sociological text, Wright uses images and motifs to embody the issues raised in the story. For example, he uses the notion of hunger here, as he does in his fiction. Here also are vivid images

LONG FICTION		NONFICTION		SCREENPLAY	
1940	Native Son	1941	Twelve Million Black Voices	1950	Native Son
1953	The Outsider	1945	Black Boy	**PLAYS**	
1954	Savage Holiday	1954	Black Power: A Record of Reactions in a Land of Pathos	1941	Native Son: The Biography of a Young American (with Paul Green)
1958	The Long Dream				
1963	Lawd Today				
1994	Rite of Passage	1956	The Color Curtain: A Report on the Bandung Conference	1968	Daddy Goodness (with Louis Sapin)
SHORT FICTION		1957	Pagan Spain		
1938	Uncle Tom's Children	1957	White Man, Listen!		
1961	Eight Men	1977	American Hunger		

of Wright's imprisonment, his entrapment in worlds he neither created nor desired. Finally, however, there is the story of his self-creation, particularly as a writer, which details how Wright inscribes himself, as in the note to the librarian, or writes his way to freedom. As he says in the final paragraph of the text, he will continue to "hurl words" at the world. Wright the writer creates the freedom that allows him to escape the oppression into which he was born.

SOURCES FOR FURTHER STUDY

Felgar, Robert, ed. *Understanding Richard Wright's "Black Boy": A Student Casebook to Issues, Sources, and Historical Documents.* Westport, Conn.: Greenwood Press, 1998.

Hakutani, Yoshinobu. "Racial Discourse and Self-Creation: Richard Wright's *Black Boy.*" In *Teaching American Ethnic Literatures*, edited by John R. Maitino and David R. Peck. Albuquerque: University of New Mexico Press, 1996.

Stepto, Robert B. *From Behind the Veil: A Study of Afro-American Narrative.* Urbana: University of Illinois Press, 1979.

NATIVE SON

Genre: Novel
Subgenre: Social protest
Published: New York, 1940
Time period: 1930s
Setting: Chicago, Illinois

Themes and Issues. Wright wrote in a preface to *Native Son* that after the publication of *Uncle Tom's Children*, "I found that I had written a book which even bankers' daughters could read and weep over and feel good about. I swore to myself that if I ever wrote another book, no one would weep over it; that it would be so hard and deep that they would have to face it without the consolation of tears." *Native Son* fulfills Wright's promise. It deals with many of the same issues in his earlier short stories—flight, violence, death—but without compromise. After the publication of *Native Son*, an immediate best-seller in 1940, it was no longer possible to pretend that the United States could escape the consequences of its racial history. Wright forced the reading public to face the inner-city conditions of its African American citizenry and its complicity in the creation of characters such as Bigger Thomas.

The Plot. The novel is divided into three books: "Fear," "Flight," and "Fate." Book 1 opens in the rat-infested apartment of Bigger Thomas, his brother, sister, and mother. The characters here are trapped in their poverty, and few avenues are open for escape. Bigger has one chance, a job with the white Dalton family, for whom he has been hired as a chauffeur. Mr. Dalton is a rich white liberal, as is his blind wife. Their daughter, Mary, is flirting with radicalism and forces Bigger to drive her and her communist boyfriend to a black restaurant, where Bigger feels uncomfortable. When Bigger drives the drunk Mary home and tries to put her in her bed, he fears discovery and accidentally suffocates her. Fearing for his own life, he decapitates Mary's corpse and puts it in the basement furnace with the naïve notion that he can destroy the evidence.

In book 2, "Flight," Bigger has a momentary feeling of power, before he is trapped by multiple forces. He flees, tries to extort money from the Daltons, and then murders his girlfriend and accomplice, Bessie, and throws her body down the airshaft of an abandoned building. Book 3, "Fate," is given over to Bigger's capture and trial. The courtroom scenes slow the momentum of the novel, as Boris Max, the communist lawyer who defends Bigger, lays out an elaborate explanation of the forces that caused Bigger to kill. Bigger, however, affirms his act as one of self-creation, saying to Max in their final meeting at the very end of the novel, "What I killed for must've been good!"

Analysis. Few novels have had such social impact as *Native Son*. The African American novelist James Baldwin called it "the most powerful and celebrated statement we have had yet of what it means to be a Negro in America." There is a raw power to the novel, particularly its first two books. Max's arguments in book 3 are necessary, for they provide the ideological underpinning for the analyses the novel makes. In the tradition of Fyodor Dostoyevski's novel *Crime and Punishment* (1866), Wright shows Bigger Thomas as self-created by his horrible act. After his first crime, he gains a sense of power and identity: "Never had his will been so free as in this night and day of fear and murder and flight." Max, in front of the jury, agrees with Bigger: "It was the first full act of his life; it was the most meaningful, exciting, and stirring thing that had ever happened to him . . . it made him free, gave him the possibility of choice, of action. . . ." In Max's larger Marxist analysis of a racist society, he goes on to blame the American "oppression" that all blacks suffer. According to Max, Bigger killed as he had lived; therefore, *His very existence is a crime against the state!"*

Wright forces readers to confront this horrible truth by making Bigger not a sympathetic hero but rather a brutal killer. He rapes and then murders Bessie, and there is no way to excuse those acts or to feel "pity" for their perpetrator. As in the "blindness" of the wealthy Mrs. Dalton, Wright forces readers to confront the horrible truths of the tragic consequences of of the oppression of African Americans .

SOURCES FOR FURTHER STUDY

Bloom, Harold, ed. *Richard Wright's "Native Son."* New York: Chelsea House, 1995.

Kinnamon, Keneth, ed. *Critical Essays on Richard Wright's "Native Son."* New York: G. K. Hall, 1997.

Miller, James A., ed. *Approaches to Teaching Wright's "Native Son."* New York: Modern Language Association, 1997

The actor Canada Lee portrayed Bigger Thomas in a dramatization of *Native Son.* Wright adapted the work for the stage in 1941 and also wrote a screenplay of his novel in 1950.

UNCLE TOM'S CHILDREN
Genre: Short stories
Subgenre: Social protest
Published: New York, 1938
Time period: 1920s and 1930s
Setting: Southern United States

Themes and Issues. *Uncle Tom's Children* was subtitled *Four Novellas* when it was first published in 1938 and won the $500 Federal

Writers' Project prize. The following year, the book was republished with the addition of a fifth and final story, "Bright and Morning Star," and a prefatory essay, "The Ethics of Living Jim Crow," which had originally appeared in the WPA collection *American Stuff* in 1937 and which Wright would reinsert in his autobiography *Black Boy* six years later. It is this second edition of *Uncle Tom's Children*, five stories and an autobiographical preface, that has been reprinted since.

Wright's first collection of short stories, and his first of more than twenty books, reveals many of the themes that he would explore throughout his work. The half-dozen pieces in this collection poignantly render the conditions of oppression and violence under which southern blacks were forced to live in the early decades of the twentieth century. In this sense, *Uncle Tom's Children* can be called the beginning of modern black protest literature.

No modern African American writer had written with such outrage about the oppression of African Americans. Zora Neale Hurston, Wright's most talented contemporary, for example, attacked the book in a review in the *Saturday Review of Literature* for its description of what she called "the Dismal Swamp of race hatred." The title of Wright's collection recalls Harriet Beecher Stowe's popular *Uncle Tom's Cabin* (1851), but nearly a century has passed, and Uncle Tom's "children" are hardly as passive as their distant relation. The stories in the collection depict victims answering violence with violence and characters moving from victimization to self-assertion and even victory.

The Plot. If there is a thread that ties the five stories together it is survival, as the protagonists attempt to stay alive in a violent, racist world. In "Big Boy Leaves Home," probably the best of the five stories, the title character and his three friends are swimming naked in a pond in the woods when a white couple stumbles upon them. The white man kills two of the youths before Big Boy kills the man in self-defense and flees with his remaining friend, Bobo. Later, from a hole where he is hiding, Big Boy sees Bobo burned alive and then escapes in a truck going north.

"Down by the Riverside" also depicts death, not by fire but by

The threat and fear of violence are ever present in *Uncle Tom's Children*. The senseless murder of blacks at the hands of whites was common in the South. Louis Lozowick's 1936 rendering *Lynching* (Smithsonian American Art Museum) captures the horror of such a scene.

flood. The black protagonist is shot when he tries to flee the soldiers guarding the river levee. In "Long Black Song," a young black mother is seduced by a white traveling salesman. Her husband kills the salesman and is then killed himself in a fire that other whites set, but not before shooting several members of the mob that pursues him. "Fire and Cloud" shifts the focus upward, describing the Reverend Dan Taylor leading a protest march demanding food for his starving parishioners in a small southern city; the story ends not in death but in triumph.

"Bright and Morning Star," the fifth and final story added in the second edition of *Uncle Tom's Children*, also describes resistance. In it, the mother of a man being tortured for his political activism kills a black informer. She is then killed along with her son by the whites who oppose their politics. In each of the stories, African Americans suffer under intolerable conditions, trying to survive the violence visited upon them by whites. In the first two stories they flee, but in the final three they stand and fight.

Analysis. The stories in *Uncle Tom's Children* are tied together by both themes and motifs, as well as by the prefatory "Ethics of Living Jim Crow." This autobiographical essay relates a number of violent incidents that Wright witnessed in his own southern boyhood and lays out the fight for survival that many of the characters in the following stories will undertake.

At the center of each story in the collection is a brutal wrong allowed by southern "Jim Crow" laws or customs that drives the protagonist to flight or martyrdom. In four of the five stories, a black man is killed by whites. The characters are victims in all of the stories, but there is a progression in the collection: The boys in "Big Boy Leaves Home" flee from their oppressors, but in later stories, grown men and women struggle to stand and resist the racism of their societies, even if it means their martyrdom. This progression is also found in *Native Son*. The stories are further unified by the motifs of music, fire, and water and by images of hunger and entrapment.

SOURCES FOR FURTHER STUDY

Gardner, Laurel J. "The Progression of Meaning in the Images of Violence in Richard Wright's *Uncle Tom's Children*." *College Language Association Journal* 38 (June 1995): 420–440.

Giles, James R. "Richard Wright's Successful Failure: A New Look at *Uncle Tom's Children*." *Phylon* 34 (September 1973): 256–266.

JanMohamed, Abdul. "Function of Death in *Uncle Tom's Children*." In *Richard Wright*, edited by Harold Bloom. New York: Chelsea House, 1987.

Other Works

EIGHT MEN (1961). Readers of Richard Wright's second collection of short fiction, published in the year following his death, were also disappointed at its appearance. However, the collection contains two stories that critics now consider among Wright's best, "The Man Who Was Almost a Man," sometimes known as "Almos' a Man," and "The Man Who Lived Underground." In the first, Dave, a seventeen-year-old African American boy in the rural South, pesters his mother until she gives him two dollars to buy a pistol, which then misfires and kills the mule that he uses to plow. Condemned to years of indentured sharecropping by the accident, Dave flees to the railroad and the North. The story carries several of Wright's major concerns: the oppression of black southern life, the flight from it, and the psychosexual dynamic that so often defines racial relations (Dave sees the gun as power and as a way of becoming a "man"). "The Man Who Was Almost a Man" has been anthologized more frequently than any other Wright story.

In William H. Johnson's 1944 painting *Moon over Harlem* (Smithsonian American Art Museum, Washington, D.C.), the police arrive to discover the aftermath of a violent incident. Wright's posthumous story collection, *Eight Men,* explores similar themes of crime, pursuit, and flight.

"The Man Who Lived Underground" is a novella of over sixty pages that was originally published in *Accent* magazine in 1942. It has drawn more attention than most of Wright's other stories and is considered by many of his critics to be his finest work. "The Man Who Lived Underground" concerns a young man named Fred Daniels, who is falsely accused of murder and escapes the police through a sewer. The story represents Wright's naturalistic technique by showing a character trapped in his environment, but in its deeply surreal and symbolic setting the story predicts Wright's own existentialist writing a decade later and anticipates Ralph Ellison's *The Invisible Man*

(1952) and other postmodernist works. *Eight Men* is notable for the inclusion of its first two stories, even though the others in the collection are not similarly powerful.

THE OUTSIDER (1953). Readers of the 1940s best-seller *Native Son* waited more than a decade for Wright's second novel, but many of them were disappointed. By the time of *The Outsider*'s publication, Wright had been living in exile in France for almost six years; he was clearly out of touch with his native country, in which he set his novel. Wright was living in the intellectually rich environment of Paris, and that influence appears as well. The novel

Though disappointing to some, *The Outsider* explored Wright's signature themes: the search for identity and the mixed blessing of freedom.

told in five sections ("Dread," "Dream," "Descent," "Despair," and "Decision") and follows the story of Cross Damon, a Chicago postal clerk with multiple legal, financial, and marital problems. He walks away from a subway wreck where he is believed to have been killed and begins a new life—of murder and communism. In the end he himself is killed, supposedly by agents of the Communist Party. *Native Son*'s mix of idea and action is used in this novel as well. The concept of freedom, so important to that first novel, is an issue here, as the protagonist tries to carve his essence out of his meaningless existence. However, the melodramatic events surrounding this struggle render the idea less effective. *The*

strongly resembles Albert Camus's *L'Étranger* (1942; *The Stranger*, 1946). The story is *Outsider*, in short, is *Native Son* with less emotional passion and literary power.

Resources

The Richard Wright papers are held in the Beinecke Rare Book Room and Manuscript Library at Yale University. Other Wright manuscripts may be found at the Northwestern, Kent State, and Harvard University libraries and at the American Library in Paris. One of the best resources for researching African American writers is the Schomburg Center for Research in Black Culture at the New York Public Library. In addition to magazines and newspapers containing Wright's work, the Schomburg Center has unmatched collections of books, films, and photographs documenting African American life. Other sources of interest and information for students of Richard Wright include the following:

Richard Wright Papers. The collection of Wright's papers held by the Beinecke Rare Book Room and Manuscript Library at Yale University is catalogued on line, with administrative, descriptive, and biographical notes. (http://webtext.library.yale.edu/sgml2html/beinecke.wright.sgm.html)

The Mississippi Writers Page: Richard Wright (1908–1960). The best Web site for complete Wright materials is the Mississippi Writers Page, which includes a brief biography; lists of publications, criticism, and media adaptations; and several useful Web links. (http://www.olemiss.edu/depts/english/mswriters/ir/wright_richard/)

Black Boy. A film version of Wright's autobiography *Black Boy* was broadcast on the PBS network on September 4, 1995, the eighty-seventh anniversary of Wright's birth. PBS maintains a fairly extensive Web site of background materials and bibliographies relating to the autobiography. (http://www.pbs.org/rwbb/rwtoc.html)

Voice of the Shuttle. The English department at the University of California, Santa Barbara, maintains a meta-Web site called "Voice of the Shuttle," with bibliographies of English and American literature. Under the "Minority Literatures/Afro-American" headings are several sites devoted to Richard Wright. (http://vos.ucsb.edu/shuttle/eng-min.html#afro-american)

DAVID PECK

Paul Zindel

BORN: May 15, 1936, Staten Island, New York
IDENTIFICATION: Late-twentieth-century New York dramatist and author of young adult fiction.

Paul Zindel's plays, especially the Pulitzer Prize–winning *The Effect of Gamma Rays on Man-in-the-Moon Marigolds* (1965), are admired for their depictions of dysfunctional families and psychological torment. His influential and controversial young adult fiction, beginning with 1968's *The Pigman*, is marked by its realism and faithfulness to the anxieties faced by adolescents. Many of Zindel's novels are critically acclaimed, and all remain popular among young readers. Zindel draws from his own troubled childhood and from his ten years of high school teaching to poignantly portray the loneliness, alienation, and confusion of young adulthood. After winning the Pulitzer Prize, Zindel found success as a scriptwriter for film and television, and many of his plays continue to be produced on stage, television, and film.

Paul Zindel was born on May 15, 1936, on Staten Island, New York. He and his sister were named after their parents, Paul and Beatrice Zindel.

When Zindel was two years old, his father abandoned the family to live with another woman, and Zindel always resented his father for his emotional and financial neglect. Zindel's mother supported the family with various jobs, working as an unlicensed real estate broker, a collie breeder, and a hot dog vendor. What influenced Zindel most was his mother's career as a practical nurse who boarded deathbed patients, a situation that meant living with terminally ill strangers. Zindel's complex yet caring mother distrusted everybody and taught her children to do the same. Zindel based many of his fictional characters on his mother.

Childhood. His family moved often, so Zindel could never maintain long-standing friendships. He felt lonely, worthless, and desperate and dared to articulate his true feelings only in secret. He has attributed his becoming a writer to this private mental life. His hobbies reflected his solitude: He designed marionettes, aquariums, and terrariums.

At the age of fifteen, Zindel contracted tuberculosis and spent eighteen months convalescing in a sanatorium. While other teenagers were forming relationships in school, Zindel was surrounded by diseased and dying adults. This experience accounts for the loneliness and alienation that pervades Zindel's work.

The Future Writer. Zindel had been writing small plays for some years. After returning to school, he demonstrated his macabre sense of humor by rewriting the early-nineteenth-century British mystery writer W. W. Jacobs's classic horror story "The Monkey's Paw." He wrote his first original play, a full-length drama about a

A view of Richmond Terrace in Staten Island, around the time the Zindels lived in the New York City borough. Estranged from his father, Paul's early years were marked by solitude and economic instability.

pianist who recovers from a dreadful disease, for a playwriting contest sponsored by the American Cancer Society and won a silver ballpoint pen.

In his senior year, Zindel succumbed to depression and despair. He ran away to Miami, Florida, and tried unsuccessfully to get a job at the *Miami News*. Too young and too unskilled to be a professional writer, he returned home disappointed and uncertain about what to do next.

College Years. Zindel attended Wagner College of Staten Island, where he majored in chemistry. He earned his bachelor's degree in chemistry in 1958 and his master's the following year. At Wagner, he enjoyed editing the school newspaper and tried to change his major to literature, but the school would not allow him to change tracks. The budding playwright inside him would not be denied, however, and Zindel took several classes in drama. His career was determined when he took a creative-writing course taught by the award-winning American dramatist Edward Albee. With Albee as mentor, he wrote his second original play, *Dimensions of Peacocks* (1959), about a teenager whose mother, a nurse, steals from patients in the hospital.

The Fledgling Playwright. At the age of twenty-four, Zindel saw a professionally produced play for the first time: Lillian Hellman's *Toys in the Attic* (1960). For him it was like a religious experience, and he began attending the theater as often as he could. From 1959 to 1969, Zindel taught chemistry at Staten Island's Tottenville High School and spent his summers writing plays. His teaching experiences gave him plenty of material.

Paul Zindel appears at a book signing. The once-struggling writer found that his appearances drew lines of fans, old and young alike.

His first two plays received little attention, but in 1963, at the age of twenty-five, he wrote *The Effect of Gamma Rays on Man-in-the-Moon Marigolds*. It premiered at the Alley Theatre in May 1965 in Houston, Texas. In 1966 Zindel won a Ford Foundation Theater Fellowship to work as playwright-in-residence at the Alley Theatre, where he learned to produce plays.

When Zindel returned to teach in New York, he realized that his students were bored at school, and many were under the influence of drugs. He felt unable to help them and quit teaching to write full-time.

The Playwright Becomes a Novelist. In 1966 National Educational Television (NET) produced a televised version of *The Effect of Gamma Rays on Man-in-the-Moon Marigolds*. Zindel was gratified when his mother watched it and loved it. Charlotte Zolotow, an editor at Harper & Row, also saw the program and was so impressed that she contacted Zindel and persuaded him to write young adult fiction. Flattered, Zindel agreed.

The Zindel family in the late 1970s. The renowned writer of books for children found himself with two of his own.

won the New York Drama Critics Circle Award and other awards and then moved to Broadway, where it won the Pulitzer Prize in 1971. Sudden fame and financial success, combined with the depression he experienced after his mother's death, proved traumatic for Zindel. He began drinking and entered a period of depression when a 1971 Broadway production of his play *And Miss Reardon Drinks a Little*, previously staged in Los Angeles in 1967, received mixed reviews. He consulted a psychotherapist to help him cope with the terrible pain, fear, and stress from which he was suffering.

Marriage and Domestic Life. Zindel met Bonnie Hildebrand when she was working as publicity director at the Cleveland Playhouse, which was staging *The Effect of Gamma Rays on Man-in-the-Moon Marigolds*. Like Zindel, Bonnie was a New Yorker, came from a broken family, and had lost her mother to cancer. They fell in love and married on October 25, 1973.

In 1974 the couple's son, David, was born. Zindel was happy to be a father, but old fears and stress led to another breakdown in his health. In 1976 the couple's daughter, Lizabeth, was born. Two years later the family moved to California so that Zindel could write screenplays in Hollywood.

Zindel felt that California was not good for him. He lived in a neighborhood filled with celebrities and sent his children to the best schools, but he felt that the honesty and raw emotion that fueled his writing were becoming corrupted by his pursuit of money. In the early 1980s, the family returned to New York, where Zindel was happy to get back to writing novels and plays that truly expressed his values and his artistic integrity.

Throughout the 1990s Zindel taught and lectured about writing, accepting invitations to speak at various schools and events and a faculty position at the University of Southern California's Professional Writing Program. He gave speeches at conferences such as the Assembly on Literature for Adolescents' Annual Convention and conducted seminars at the American Embassy School in New Delhi, India.

Zindel read several young adult novels and found that most were fluffy stories of the Nancy Drew and Hardy Boys variety. He felt it unjust that fiction for teens did not discuss the real issues and problems of adolescence. Zindel remembered his students and set out to depict teenagers who drank, smoked, were sexually active, and disliked school.

In 1968 Zindel published his first novel, *The Pigman*, to the delight of both critics and adolescent readers. That same year, Zindel's mother died of cancer. Because of their stormy relationship, Zindel accepted her death with both grief and relief. He was glad, at least, that she had witnessed some of his success as a writer. Zindel's second book, *My Darling, My Hamburger* (1969), was also a huge success, so he determined to continue writing novels.

In 1970 *The Effect of Gamma Rays on Man-in-the-Moon Marigolds* premiered off Broadway and

The Writer's Work

Paul Zindel has written plays, novels, screenplays, and teleplays. He is most famous for his play *The Effect of Gamma Rays on Man-in-the-Moon Marigolds* and for his young adult novels. Critics sometimes criticize his outrageous imagination, but teenagers enjoy the fast-paced action, black comedy, and realism of his stories.

Issues in Zindel's Work.
Zindel depicts adolescents' true feelings about classmates and parents. His adult characters rarely offer compassion or assistance when it is most needed. Zindel's teenagers rebel through sexual activity and delinquent behavior but eventually gain self-esteem. Zindel's stories for middle school children, including 1993's *Fright Party* and *Attack of the Killer Fishsticks* and 1994's *City Safari* and *The 100% Laugh Riot*, deal with themes such as bullying and popularity in school.

Zindel's fiction veered into the fantastic in the 1990s, with the publication of such young adult novels as *Loch* (1994), about a brother and sister who find prehistoric creatures in a Vermont lake; *Raptor* (1998), in which two boys discover a living dinosaur; and *Rats* (1999), in which mutant rats infest Staten Island.

People in Zindel's Work.
The parent and teacher characters in Zindel's works are usually moody, dishonest, abusive, or distant. His discouraged and alienated teens must solve their problems without adult help and usually end up in an escalating series of troubles.

For example, in *Pardon Me, You're Stepping on My Eyeball!* (1976), two disturbed teenagers feel psychologically imprisoned. Marsh suffers mistreatment from his alcoholic mother and guilt over an accident that killed his father, so he becomes a pathological liar. Edna's domineering parents make her feel worthless. On a crazy midnight drive, the two wreck their car, throw Marsh's father's ashes over a cliff, and set off fireworks to symbolize their independence and repentance. In *David and Della* (1993), a

struggling teenage playwright is unfortunately attracted to a flamboyant, alcoholic actress. These characters are drawn in part from Zindel's image of himself as a teenager.

The Themes of Alienation and Friendship.
Zindel's protagonists rarely have "normal," loving families, so they cannot form healthy relationships with other teens. His high school students hate their teachers and their apparently meaningless lessons. His teens drift from one crisis to another without guidance, without knowing what they want, without envisioning a happy future.

Success was always important to Paul Zindel but not at the expense of personal happiness. This photograph was taken in 1983, a time when the writer realized he needed to go home, back to New York and a less status-obsessed life.

Prehistoric creatures still living in the present feature strongly in the fiction Zindel produced in the 1990s. Christian Pierre's 1995 artwork *Rainbow Bronto* captures these fantastic, often whimsical visitors from another time.

Adolescents need love, security, and friendship. If they do not receive these at home, they may find other unhappy peers or follow troublemaking bullies. In Zindel's stories, teens fall into frightening situations, grapple with them in their different ways, and learn important lessons about loyalty, responsibility, and caring. Although critics call Zindel's novels bleak, his stories end on upbeat notes, with adolescents gaining wisdom and self-respect.

Zindel and Film. Many of Zindel's plays have been filmed and televised. A television production of *The Effect of Gamma Rays on Man-in-the-Moon Marigolds* was sponsored by National Educational Television (NET) in 1966, and a film version was produced by Twentieth Century-Fox in 1973. A 1966 television production of Zindel's play *Let Me Hear You Whisper* portrays a cleaning woman at a science lab who, unlike the scientists, develops a loving friendship with a dolphin.

Zindel's adaptations include the 1972 Warner Bros. film *Up the Sandbox*, based on Anne Roiphe's novel about a housewife who fantasizes an adventurous life, and the 1974 Warner Bros. film *Mame*, based on the memoir *Auntie Mame* by Patrick Dennis. *Maria's Lovers*, released by Cannon Films in 1984, portrays the unhappy marriage of a military veteran and his childhood sweetheart.

Among Zindel's televised movies are his adaptations of Lewis Carroll's *Alice in Wonderland* (1985); *Babes in Toyland* (1986), starring Drew Barrymore and Keanu Reeves; and Mark Twain's *A Connecticut Yankee in King Arthur's Court* (1989).

Zindel's Literary Legacy. The groundbreaking significance of Zindel's work lies in its realistic treatment of teenagers' concerns. Before Zindel, few authors depicted adolescent rebelliousness, contemporary slang, the tedium of school, unkind parents, or experimentation with

SOME INSPIRATIONS BEHIND ZINDEL'S WORK

Because his parents never kept books in the house, Paul Zindel's literary temperament grew from daydreaming during his unhappy childhood. That difficult period forced him to look inward for ways to escape.

The dramatist Edward Albee encouraged Zindel to write, and a college friend, actor John Foster, introduced him to New York's theatrical scene. The poignant and brutal works of the American playwrights Lillian Hellman and Tennessee Williams influenced Zindel's style and themes.

Zindel often bases characters on people he knew in his life. Adults may be absent, as his father was, or neurotic, like his mother; his teens suffer anger and depression as he and his sister did. He also draws upon the students he taught, portraying likeable or obnoxious personalities who are lonely, vulnerable, mischievous, pretentious, flashy, or self-destructive.

The esteemed American dramatist Edward Albee was a strong influence on Zindel, helping the young writer discover his love of playwriting.

Zindel's adaptation of Lewis Carroll's *Alice in Wonderland* was made into a two-part, four-hour television miniseries in the 1980s. Sammy Davis Jr. played the role of the Caterpillar.

sex and drugs. Zindel's popular books have remained continually in print since their original publications.

Zindel's plays are noted for their examination of neurotic adults, mostly women. Many actresses are grateful to Zindel for writing so many rich, gritty roles for women. His plays have continued to be performed in high school, college, and regional repertory productions.

BIBLIOGRAPHY

DiGaetani, John L. *A Search for a Postmodern Theater: Interviews with Contemporary Playwrights*. New York: Greenwood Press, 1991.

Donelson, Kenneth L., and Alleen Pace Nilsen, eds. *Literature for Today's Young Adults*. Glenview, Ill.: Scott Foresman, 1980.

Drew, Bernard A. "Paul Zindel." In *The One Hundred Most Popular Young Adult Authors: Biographical Sketches and Bibliographies*. Englewood, Colo.: Libraries Unlimited, 1996.

Forman, Jack Jacob. *Presenting Paul Zindel*. Boston: Twayne Publishers, 1988.

Hall, Peggy. *"The Effect of Gamma Rays on Man-in-the-Moon Marigolds" by Paul Zindel: Study Guide*. Palatine, Ill.: Novel Units, 1989.

Rees, David. *The Marble in the Water: Essays on Contemporary Writers of Fiction for Children and Young Adults*. Boston: Horn Book, 1980.

Vick, Diane. *Favorite Authors of Young Adult Fiction*. Torrance, Calif.: F. Schaffer, 1995.

Ward, Martha E., and Dorothy A. Marquardt. *Authors of Books for Young People*. Metuchen, N.J.: Scarecrow Press, 1971.

Reader's Guide to Major Works

THE EFFECT OF GAMMA RAYS ON MAN-IN-THE-MOON-MARIGOLDS

Genre: Play
Subgenre: Bourgeois drama
Produced: Texas, 1965
Time period: 1960s
Setting: Hunsdorfers' house

Themes and Issues. Paul Zindel's play is autobiographical. The tension between the adolescent Tillie and her crazy mother Beatrice is based on Zindel's experience with his own mother, although the play's Beatrice is far crueler than her model. Beatrice's anger and frustration are generated by despair and a disappointed life. Tillie's older sister, Ruth, is alternately spoiled and punished by Beatrice and is growing up to become just like her. Tillie, however, wants to dream her own dreams and to live her own life and must find a way to escape her mother's insanity.

The themes of *The Effect of Gamma Rays on Man-in-the-Moon Marigolds* are presented as a collection of contrasts: the beauty and awe to be found in the rational world of science versus the ugliness and hatred within irrational human minds; the love and care Tillie and Ruth lavish on their pet rabbit versus the emotional neglect they experience from their mother; hopes and dreams versus bitter resignation; mental chains versus spiritual liberation. Tillie's rebellion is a positive thing. She refuses to accept her mother's low opinion of her. With her science teacher as a mentor, she accomplishes something she can be proud of, and she realizes that she can overcome the neuroses in her household.

The Plot. A high school student, Tillie Hunsdorfer, lives in a ramshackle house with her epileptic older sister, Ruth, and her mother, Beatrice, an impractical, embittered widow who earns money by nursing an elderly invalid. Alternately charming, self-absorbed, and abusive, Beatrice wreaks petty vengeance on everyone around her, tormenting her daughters with furious outbursts, such as threats to kill their pet rabbit. Although they obey Beatrice, Ruth and Tillie have reached the age where they want to establish their own identities. Ruth is prettier than Tillie, but she is malicious and has seizures whenever she experiences strong emotions.

The opening act establishes the very different mental worlds inhabited by Tillie and the rest of her family. Tillie, speaking in darkness, evokes awe and wonder with a monologue about her hand, whose atoms were originally created in the fire of stars even before the solar system was formed. As the lights come up, Beatrice unpleasantly breaks the spell with a nasty phone conversation with Tillie's science teacher and then with a cruel order for Tillie to miss school.

Tillie is devastated, as she was anticipating an experiment in science class. She tries to explain atomic half-life to her mother, but Beatrice ignores her, turning the discussion into an insulting series of wordplays on the meaning of the phrase "half-life." Beatrice cannot stand to see her daughter enjoying something. At school, Tillie is an outcast: plain, shy, and eccentric. She lives for her science class and devotes herself to a project involving marigold seeds exposed to varying levels of radiation.

The play reaches its climax in act 2, when Tillie is chosen as a finalist for a science fair contest. The Hunsdorfers are preparing to go to the science fair, when Beatrice announces that Ruth must stay home. Ruth throws a tantrum, screaming out "Betty the Loon," which is what the town gossips once called Beatrice. Her mother breaks down, and Ruth triumphantly goes with Tillie.

At the science fair, after another student's presentation, Tillie explains the outcome of her project to the audience. Gamma rays will kill

In this scene from the film version of *The Effect of Gamma Rays on Man-in-the-Moon Marigolds,* Beatrice, played by Joanne Woodward, comforts her epileptic daughter Ruth. The bright, precocious Tillie looks on, relegated to the edge of her family.

Effect of Gamma Rays on Man-in-the-Moon Marigolds offers heart-rending drama in its familial conflicts, along with poetic moments of beauty and hope.

Tillie's science experiment bears a thematic parallel to her own life. The radiation of the seeds symbolizes the domestic and social environments in which people are raised. Some will be warped and become sociopathic or neurotic, as suggested by the mutated marigolds, but some will emerge stronger, having coped with their hardships.

Although Zindel has noted that American society has overvalued science and technology at the cost of more humanitarian and spiritual concerns, his play does present a positive view of science, suggesting that it offers a beautiful and marvelous view of the universe. Zindel believes there is some underlying meaning to the universe, and his play presents a wonderful contrast between the magic and majesty of the cosmos and the shabby, squalid lives in which some unhappy individuals reside. *The Effect of Gamma Rays on Man-in-the-Moon Marigolds* also argues that following one's dream can lead to self-esteem and self-reliance, despite an apparently unendurable environment.

The Effect of Gamma Rays on Man-in-the-Moon Marigolds ran on Broadway for 819 performances from 1970 to 1972. It won the Pulitzer Prize, the New York Drama Critics Circle Award for best American play, an Obie Award for the best off–Broadway play, and the Vernon Rice Drama Desk Award. Further, in 1971 Zindel received an honorary doctorate from his alma mater, Wagner College.

some marigold seeds, but others will mutate, and some will actually live and thrive. She finally earns respect from her peers by winning the competition.

However, in her fury at Ruth and in her intense jealousy of Tillie's success, Beatrice retaliates against her children by chloroforming their rabbit. When Tillie and Ruth return home, they find Beatrice drunk and the rabbit dead. Despite this latest trauma, the pride, self-esteem, and great joy that Tillie finds in her victory helps her to survive her difficult childhood.

Analysis. Zindel's two-act play is reminiscent of Tennessee Williams's *The Glass Menagerie* (1944), a story of a dysfunctional family with a handicapped daughter who dreams of being valued and loved. Like Williams's play, *The*

SOURCES FOR FURTHER STUDY

Bonin, Jane F. *Prize-Winning American Drama: A Bibliographical and Descriptive Guide*. Metuchen, N.J.: Scarecrow Press, 1973.

HIGHLIGHTS IN ZINDEL'S LIFE

1936   Paul Zindel is born on May 15 on Staten Island, New York.

1951   Contracts tuberculosis and convalesces in a sanatorium.

1958   Earns a bachelor's degree in chemistry from Wagner College on Staten Island.

1959   Earns a master's degree in chemistry from Wagner College.

1965   *The Effect of Gamma Rays on Man-in-the-Moon Marigolds* premieres in Houston, Texas.

1966   Zindel receives Ford Foundation Theater Fellowship; spends a year in Texas producing high school plays.

1968   Publishes his first novel for young adults, *The Pigman*; his mother dies.

1971   Zindel wins the Pulitzer Prize for drama for *The Effect of Gamma Rays Man-in-the-Moon Marigolds.*

1973   Joins Actors Studio in New York; marries Bonnie Hildebrand.

1974   Son, David, is born.

1976   Daughter, Lizabeth, is born.

1978   The Zindels move to California.

1981   The Zindels return to New York.

1990   Zindel begins teaching at the University of Southern California.

Forman, Jack Jacob. *Presenting Paul Zindel*. Boston: Twayne Publishers, 1988.

Miner, M. D. "Grotesque Drama in the 70s." *Kansas Quarterly* 12, no. 4 (1980).

THE PIGMAN

Genre: Novel

Subgenre: Young adult fiction

Published: New York, 1968

Time period: 1960s

Setting: Franklin High School in poor urban setting

Themes and Issues. Zindel's first novel is disturbing and tragic. Two high school friends, John and Lorraine, befriend an elderly man, who offers them love and the run of his house. Through their unthinking carelessness, they ruin both his house and his life. The themes of the novel include the importance of love and friendship, the necessity of repaying kindness with kindness, and the consequences of selfish and inconsiderate behavior. John and Lorraine come away from their relationship with Mr. Pignati feeling guilt and sorrow. They also come to understand that one must deal with all people honestly and responsibly—and without delinquent behavior—including their instable parents and the other students who have refused their friendship.

The Plot. In alternating chapters, John and Lorraine each give a first-person account of their friendship with the strange and reclusive Mr. Pignati. They start to spend time after school with the Pigman, so nicknamed because of his precious collection of glass, ceramic, and marble pigs. He loves these pigs because they remind him of his wife; in a disturbing scene, John and Lorraine find evidence that his wife is not away, as Mr. Pignati has told them, but dead. They feel pity for his psychological denial of her death. During the next few months, the three friends shop in Manhattan and go to the zoo, where Mr. Pignati daily visits a baboon of which he is fond.

When Mr. Pignati is hospitalized for a heart attack—caused in part by the antics of his young friends—he gives them the keys to his house. John and Lorraine spend more and more time there and eventually decide to

---

PLAYS

1959 Dimensions of Peacocks
1960 Euthanasia and the Endless Hearts
1964 A Dream of Swallows
1965 The Effect of Gamma Rays on Man-in-the-Moon Marigolds
1967 And Miss Reardon Drinks a Little
1972 The Secret Affairs of Mildred Wild
1973 Let Me Hear You Whisper and The Ladies Should Be in Bed: Two Plays
1975 Ladies at the Alamo
1983 A Destiny with Half Moon Street
1989 Amulets Against the Dragon Forces
1996 Every Seventeen Minutes the Crowd Goes Crazy!

LONG FICTION

1968 The Pigman
1969 My Darling, My Hamburger
1970 I Never Loved Your Mind
1975 I Love My Mother
1976 Pardon Me, You're Stepping on My Eyeball!
1977 Confessions of a Teenage Baboon

1978 The Undertaker's Gone Bananas
1980 A Star for the Latecomer (with Bonnie Zindel)
1980 The Pigman's Legacy
1981 The Girl Who Wanted a Boy
1982 To Take a Dare (with Crescent Dragonwagon)
1984 Harry and Hortense at Hormone High
1987 The Amazing and Death-Defying Diary of Eugene Dingman
1989 A Begonia for Miss Applebaum
1993 David and Della
1993 Fright Party
1993 Attack of the Killer Fishsticks
1993 Fifth Grade Safari
1994 Loch
1994 City Safari
1994 The 100% Laugh Riot
1995 The Doom Stone
1998 Reef of Death
1998 Raptor
1999 Rats

SCREENPLAYS

1972 Up the Sandbox
1974 Mame
1984 Maria's Lovers (with Gerard Brach and Andrei Konchalovsky)

1985 Runaway Train

TELEPLAYS

1966 Let Me Hear You Whisper
1985 Alice in Wonderland (adapted from the story by Lewis Carroll)
1986 Babes in Toyland (adapted from the operetta by Victor Herbert)
1989 A Connecticut Yankee in King Arthur's Court (adapted from the novel by Mark Twain)

NONFICTION

1992 The Pigman and Me

ADULT FICTION

1984 When a Darkness Falls

PAUL ZINDEL

Author of The Pigman's Legacy

THE PIGMAN

Andy Warhol's 1979 work *Fiesta Pig* finds the farm animal placed in a domestic setting. In *The Pigman,* the collection of pigs Mr. Pignati keeps in his home becomes a symbol of grief and absence.

throw a party in the house. Unfortunately, the other high school students who show up have no respect for Mr. Pignati or for his belongings. The teens' behavior rapidly spins out of control, and a trouble-making classmate smashes the collection of pigs. At that moment, Mr. Pignati arrives home, released early from the hospital. He is horrified and grief stricken to find what has happened in his absence.

The next day John and Lorraine call Mr. Pignati to try to make amends. Mr. Pignati feels hurt by their actions, but out of the greatness of his heart, he forgives them and finally agrees to accompany them to the zoo. Tragically, the three find that Mr. Pignati's favorite baboon has died. Mr. Pignati collapses with another heart attack, this time fatal. His two friends are left to ponder the extent of their guilt.

Analysis. The setting of *The Pigman,* an urban wasteland, symbolizes the absence of humanitarian values in most of the novel's characters. John and Lorraine both come from dysfunctional families. John, the chief instigator of the story's events, feels inadequate and resentful because his parents pressure him to be more like his admired brother. John's rebellious nature leads him to drink, swear, and smoke heavily. He feels like a prisoner; on the novel's first page, he declares that he dislikes school.

Lorraine, though less adventurous, has a similarly uncomfortable home life. Her divorced mother constantly warns her that all men are sex fiends. The teens' family backgrounds are significant to the novel's themes of caring and responsibility; John and Lorraine have never been taught to behave with kindness, trustworthiness, or respect. Mr. Pignati, however, is caring, patient, and generous, the very picture of what Zindel imagines a father ought to be. As they spend time in Mr. Pignati's company, John and Lorraine realize that the world is wider and filled with more kinds of people—some of them very special—than they had imagined. They realize that their home lives are not those all people live and that they do not have to feel imprisoned forever.

The differences in their personalities lead to conflict between John and Lorraine. Lorraine is reluctant both to accept the key to Mr. Pignati's house and to throw a party there. However, she is easily swayed by John, who uses his occasional charm and good looks to manipulate her.

After Mr. Pignati's death, John and Lorraine both realize they have lost not only a good friend but also their own innocence. They understand now that they have control over their own actions and that part of growing up is accepting responsibility for their behavior. The alternating-chapter narratives serve as individual confessions about their shame and sorrow, about the lessons they learned from Mr. Pignati's playful love of life, and about their disgust with their own lives.

The Pigman became a best-seller and earned numerous honors. The book won honorary mention in the *Boston Globe-Horn Book* Awards. The Child Study Association of America selected it as a Children's Book of the Year. It is listed as one of the Notable Children's Books of 1940–1970 by the American Library Association and as one of their Best of the Best Books for Young Adults (1975). *The Pigman* sold more than one million copies and helped to establish young adult fiction as a distinct literary genre.

SOURCES FOR FURTHER STUDY

Forman, Jack Jacob. *Presenting Paul Zindel*. Boston: Twayne Publishers, 1988.

Helbig, Alethea K., and Agnes Regan Perkins. *Dictionary of American Children's Fiction, 1960–1984: Recent Books of Recognized Merit*. New York: Greenwood Press, 1986.

Weiner, Sharon. *Novel Guide for "The Pigman" by Paul Zindel*. Glenview, Ill.: Scott, Foresman, 1995.

Other Works

HARRY AND HORTENSE AT HORMONE HIGH (1984). This novel shares similarities with *The Pigman*. It is narrated by two close friends, Harry and Hortense, and re-creates the plot in which a boy and girl meet a mentally ill person with tragic consequences.

The eccentric in this novel is a new boy at school, Jason Rohr. Jason is tall and handsome but has a pathological fascination with Greek mythology. He claims to be a reincarnation of Icarus, the son of the mythical, fantastic engineer Daedalus, who built the labyrinth to imprison the Minotaur. Daedalus designed wax wings to escape slavery in Crete. Icarus, intoxicated with flying, stole his father's wings and soared too close to the sun. The wings melted, and he fell to his death. Jason, unfortunately, overlooks this part of the story.

Harry and Hortense do not really believe that Jason is a half-deity, as he insists. In fact, they discover that Jason lives in a rundown shack with his poor aunt. Investigating further, they learn that Jason's father killed his mother and then committed suicide. The instability of his home parallels Jason's mental instability. Nevertheless, the two friends need a hero and are fascinated by Jason's boasting and his self-appointed role to save the world.

The other students, though, deride and torment Jason, until in a fury he plants dynamite at the school and attempts to fly off the roof in the explosion. Harry and Hortense are horrified by this tragedy and try to find some meaning in it. They grow closer together as they decide that they will carry on Jason's mission to fight evil and improve the world.

Marc Chagall's 1975 painting *La Chute d'Icare* captures the moment when Icarus is about to plummet to the earth. In Zindel's 1984 novel, *Harry and Hortense at Hormone High,* tragedy results from a student's delusional and excessive identification with this mythological character.

His girlfriend Liz, meanwhile, does not get along with her overprotective mother and intrusive stepfather. Sean and Liz are friends with Dennis and Maggie, who are similarly sensitive and self-conscious.

Sean is dissatisfied with what he has seen of life. Disdainful of both school and his parents, he loves only Liz and frequently presses her for sexual intercourse. Zindel paints a harsh picture of just how unhelpful adults are to teenagers in dealing with the desires and fears caused by their hormones: One teacher advises that when boys start to talk about sexual topics, girls should change the subject and suggest going out to get a hamburger.

When Liz finally gives in to Sean, she becomes pregnant. Sean feels distressed about this development and offers to marry her, but Sean's father decrees that Liz must get an abortion instead. Liz feels frightened and turns to Maggie, rather than to an adult, for help. Maggie stands by her friend, and when Liz's illegal abortion is nearly fatal, Maggie saves Liz's life. In the end, the two couples go their separate ways, but all four adolescents feel that they have gained maturity through their hardship.

Harry and Hortense at Hormone High is a gripping story. Paul Zindel portrays the various students' reactions to the delusional Jason, from fascination to intolerance, with great skill. His portrait of Jason is a powerful study in despair. Zindel himself most valued the book's worthwhile belief in divinity and heroism.

MY DARLING, MY HAMBURGER (1969). If Zindel broke new ground with his first novel, he trespassed taboo territory in his second, a story about sex and abortion that critics call one of his best books. In this novel, four high-school seniors struggle with the problems of intimate relationships. Sean feels uncomfortable around his father, who is more interested in making money than in being a good dad.

THE PIGMAN AND ME (1992). Zindel's autobiography describes his own adolescence. The book's title refers to the man who, like Mr. Pignati in *The Pigman*, served as the young author's friend and mentor. The opening paragraph grabs even the most reluctant reader:

"Eight hundred and fifty-three horrifying things had happened to me by the time I was a teenager. That was when I met my Pigman, whose real name was Nonno Frankie," Zindel says, adding, "If you haven't croaked before finishing this book, then you'd understand how I survived being a teenager."

In his usual thoughtful, humorous style, Zindel remembers Frankie as his first positive male role model. Frankie's daughter, a young Italian woman named Connie Vivona, for a while lived with the Zindels. Zindel's mother soon came to dislike Connie and her hyperactive twin sons; this situation which let to conflicts and suicide threats from the unstable Mrs. Zindel. However, in the midst of dealing with family problems, bullies, cockroaches, and teenage angst, Zindel learned much sound advice and a passion for life from Frankie. This autobiography is a wonderful read that provides many insights into Zindel and his writing.

Resources

The major collection of Paul Zindel's manuscripts is held by Boston University Library's Department of Special Collections. Other sources of interest for students of Paul Zindel include the following:

CD-ROM. Paul Zindel is featured on CD 1 the *AuthorWorks* (1997) series, produced by Scott Foresman, in cooperation with the Library of Congress. This excellent interactive multimedia kit contains three CD-ROMs, three teachers' guides, and three user's guides. These IBM-compatible Microsoft Windows CD-ROMs, aimed at students in grades six through eight, contain text, photographs, slide shows, music, Quicktime movies, and spoken audio clips about authors and their times.

Computerized Instruction. Another computer resource is the *Electronic Bookshelf Titles Disk: B-94* (1996), a three-and-one-half-inch disk that contains computer-assisted instruction for Young Hoosier Book Award books, including Zindel's *The Doom Stone* (1995). The disk is available from Electronic Bookshelf of Frankfort, Indiana. An older kit, for Macintosh users, is *The Pigman* (1983), produced by Media Basics Courseware of Larchmont, New York. The package consists of a five-and-one-quarter-inch computer disk, a study guide, and two activity sheets. Written for junior and senior high students, the program evaluates the reader's level of comprehension and increases skills in critical thinking and vocabulary.

The Educational Paperback Association. This organization's Web site offers a Paul Zindel biography, a selected bibliography, and a listing of literary criticism. (http://www.edupaperback.org/authorbios/zindelpa.html)

FIONA KELLEGHAN

Index

Page numbers in **boldface** type indicate article titles. Page numbers in *italic* type indicate illustrations.